D0080882

Studies in the Modern Russian Language

GENERAL EDITOR: DENNIS WARD
Professor of Russian, University of Edinburgh

3

WORD FORMATION IN THE NOUN AND ADJECTIVE

WORD FORMATION IN THE NOUN AND ADJECTIVE

J.K.W.NORBURY

Lecturer in Russian, University of Exeter

CAMBRIDGE

AT THE UNIVERSITY PRESS

1967

Published by the Syndics of the Cambridge University Press
Bentley House, 200 Euston Road, London N.W. 1
American Branch: 32 East 57th Street, New York, N.Y. 10022

Library of Congress Catalogue Card Number: 67-10258

Printed in Great Britain
at the University Printing House, Cambridge
(Brooke Crutchley, University Printer)

CONTENTS

ACKNOWLEDGEMENT

I should like to thank Miss M. Gardiner for the care with which she typed the present work. J.N.

1

INTRODUCTION

A. *Aims and general outline*

The present work describes in detail the procedures used in the formation of nouns and adjectives in Russian and provides lists of the most common prefixes, suffixes, deaffixed stems and contracted stems used in these procedures. Word formation in Russian, as in English, may be either derivatory or non-derivatory. The derivatory techniques include affixation, composition, internal modification, stress-shift and reduplication. Non-derivatory methods include onomatopoeia, reduplication of meaningless syllables and borrowing from another language.

The work is divided into three parts. In the first of these (§§1–7) a list is given of the thirteen procedures by which the number of nouns and adjectives in Russian and English has been or is being increased. Twelve of these procedures are common to both languages. The treatment of each of the procedures used in Russian, which follows, includes a detailed description of the two most important of these, affixation-deaffixation and composition. The first part ends with a brief history of word formation in Russian and a comparison between the procedures used in English and those used in Russian.

The second part (§8) consists of a list of the affixes (prefixes and suffixes) most commonly used in Russian to form nouns and adjectives. It is recommended that the forms and functions of these affixes be learnt for active use.

The final part (§9) is an index of affixes. It includes all the morphemes discussed in §8 and contains in addition all unproductive or weakly productive morphemes that can with confidence be analysed as affixes. It is intended for reference only.

B. *The value of understanding word formation*

A knowledge of the regularly operating derivatory procedures of any language is of little or no practical value to a native speaker. As English-speakers we will be reluctant to make active use of such procedures if we have not grown used to meeting them through hearing or reading. Unless we wish to produce a special effect the knowledge that the suffix *-scape* denotes 'a variety of scenery' will not be put into active service. On the other hand, it is not necessary to formulate this information if we are to understand the little-used words *earthscape*, *moonscape*, *mindscape*, as we can guess their meaning from the familiar *landscape*. Such knowledge would, however, be found very useful by a foreign learner of English who, while perhaps possessing the English *landscape* in his vocabulary, might not have attempted to analyse its form. Most foreign learners of English do accumulate an appreciation of the functions of our affixes and of the way in which they are joined to roots and a rough idea of the ways in which compound words are made up. But this process may take nearly as long for a foreigner as it has taken for us native speakers, and, without systematic learning, there is no guarantee that serious gaps have been avoided.

The value of a knowledge of word formation is even greater in learning Russian than in learning English because of the easier application of that knowledge. Unlike English, Russian relies very little on non-formal methods of creating new words (e.g. change of grammatical class). This means that a familiarity with the most frequently used affixes and 'units of composition' (see §5 B(2)) together with a general idea of the principles of word formation in Russian is sufficient to increase the learner's passive vocabulary to an enormous extent. Attempted active word formation by a non-native cannot be recommended without reservation (as there is little regularity in semantic growth and so no guarantee of success) but it may often be employed successfully in emergencies if care is taken to use only the most productive forms (see §4 G).

C. *Word-forming procedures in English and Russian (summary)*

In examining the ways in which new words are formed in Russian we are helped to a very great extent by the existence of identical procedures in our own language. The similarities in this respect between English and Russian may be largely accounted for by the origin of the languages in mutually intelligible 'Proto-Indo-European' dialects. But some of the shared procedures, such as reduplication and shortening (usually the work of children), are common human property (Malays call the police 'mata-mata'), while the more sophisticated methods of word formation used in English and Russian are vigorously exploited in non-Indo-European languages. One type of composition (juxtaposition) is very productive in languages as geographically separate as Chinese and Finnish, and internal modification is the essential means of derivation in Hebrew and Arabic.

English and Russian, however, share more than a collection of twelve word-forming procedures. The *material* used in the most common procedures (borrowing, affixation, composition) is becoming increasingly common to both languages. Many of the units used in these procedures (whole words, affixes, roots or stems) are used in the transmission of ideas from one European language to another. They are normally of Greek or Latin origin, have frequently undergone reshaping in English or French, and are most numerous in writing on philosophy and the biological and physical sciences. That there is considerable reason to suppose that an international vocabulary is growing up in these fields will be confirmed by anybody who has heard a conversation between British and Soviet (or French, or German) scientists not fluent in the use of the language of their colleagues.

New words are created in a wide variety of ways. The methods listed below are those used by speakers of English and Russian and comprise (*a*) those by which the word stock of either language is enriched by entirely new words ('Non-derivatory procedures') and (*b*) those which to some extent use morphemes or complete words already in use in the language concerned ('Derivatory procedures'). Word-forming procedures alien to both languages (for instance, tonal differentiation, initial mutation) are excluded from the list. Numbers in brackets refer to sections or subsections where a fuller description will be found.

Non-derivatory procedures

1. Creation 'from nothing' (§2).
   Rus. ауэ, пршкхт (words used by Futurist writers and suggestive of emotions).
   Eng. *owch*, *Zixt* (a brand of soap).

2. Reduplication of meaningless syllables (§2).
   Rus. ба́ба (old woman), дя́дя (uncle).
   Eng. *geegee*, *yo-yo*.

3. Onomatopoeia (normally accompanied by suffixation in Russian) (§2).
   Rus. куку́шка (a cuckoo), хлоп (bang).
   Eng. *purr*, *plonk*.

4. Borrowing without morphological adaptation (§6).

4*a*. Borrowing with minimal phonetic adaptation.
Rus. парк (a park), стеари́н (stearin).
Eng. *park*, *centre*.

4*b*. Borrowing with such a degree of phonetic adaptation as to obscure the etymology of the word.
Rus. и́звесть (lime) (from Greek and (now) 'International' *asbestos*); верста́к (a work-bench) (from German *Werkstatt*).
Eng. *plum* (from Latin *prunum*), *flannel* (from Welsh *gwlanen*).

4*c*. Borrowing with spelling changes due to mistakes in transmission.
Rus. трюм (a ship's hold) from Dutch *t'Ruim* where the article is seen as part of the word.
Eng. *zenith* (and French *zénith*) from Arabic *zamt*, owing to copyist's error.

Derivatory procedures

5. Resemanticization (§3A).
Rus. мо́йка (для посу́ды) (a dish-washing machine; originally: the action of washing);
крестья́нин (a peasant; originally: a Christian).
Eng. *ballot* (originally: *a little ball*), *heathen* (originally: *a heath dweller*).

6. Polysemanticization (§3B).
Rus. кра́йний (when used as equivalent to после́дний), пло́ский (when used in an abstract sense).
Eng. *caravan*, *quick* (originally only = alive).

6*a*. Change of grammatical class (conversion) (§3C).
Rus. смерть (death; terribly) (used as noun or adverb);
весно́й (spring; in spring) (used as noun or adverb).
Eng. *scratch* (used as noun, adjective, verb or adverb);
like (used as noun, adjective, verb, preposition or conjunction).

7. Internal modification (§3D).
Rus. шёл (he was going) / ход-и́-л (he used to go);
вез-ти́ (to be transporting) / воз-и́-ть (to transport).
Eng. *a road* / *to ride* (noun / verb), *a stroke* / *to strike* (noun / verb).

8. Accentual (stress) distinction (§3E).
Rus. мало́ (short form of ма́л-ень-к-ое) / ма́ло (adverb and numeral);
стоя́ (gerund) / сто́я (adverb).
Eng. *minúte* (adjective) / *mínute* (noun);
súspect (noun and adjective) / *suspéct* (verb).
N.B. Internal modification and stress-shift are in certain instances functions of conversion (6*a*).

9. Reduplication of meaningful syllables (with or without change of internal vowel) (§3F).
Not used in Russian.
Eng. *zigzag* (cf. *to tack*), *knick-knack* (cf. *to knock*).

10. Affixation (§4A).

10*a*. Prefixation (§§4B, 4E, 4G, 4H).
Rus. вы́-ход (an exit), анти-америка́нский (anti-American).
Eng. *outflow*, *underhand*.

10*b*. Suffixation (§§4C, 4E, 4G, 4H).
Rus. моло́ч-н-ик (milkman) (молоко́: моло́чный, 'milk');
ви́ди-м-ый (visible) (ви́д-и-т, 'he sees').
Eng. *near-ly*, *avail-able*.

10*c*. Prefixation and suffixation (§§4B, 4E, 4G, 4H).
Rus. до-революцио́н-н-ый (pre-Revolutionary);
по-тре́б-н-ость (necessity).
Eng. *pre-revolution-ary*, *hemi-spher-ic*.

11. Deaffixation (§4D).
Rus. топь (marsh) (from топ-и́-ть, 'to sink');
за́пись (a recording) (from запис-а́-ть, 'to record').
Eng. *greed* (from *greedy*), *difficult* (from *difficulty*).

12. Compounding (composition) (§5A).

12*a*. Compounding with whole components (§§5A, 5B).
Rus. железобето́н (ferro-concrete), самоуве́ренный (self-confident).
Eng. *cupboard*, *ore-bearing*.

12*b*. Compounding with abbreviated components (contractions, 'units of composition', initials) (§§5B, 5C, 5D).
Rus. колхо́з (collective-farm, = коллекти́вное хозя́йство);
управдо́м (house-manager, = управля́ющий до́мом).
Eng. *laser* (Rus. ла́зер) (= *l*ight *a*mplification by *s*timulated *e*mission of *r*adiation).

13. Shortening without change in meaning.
Rus. зав (manager, = заве́дующий), пом (assistant, = помо́щник).
Eng. *fray* (= *affray*).

2

NON-DERIVATORY PROCEDURES

Non-derived words need not occupy us for long as they are very few in number and of complex and confused origin. The sources of these words are the same for Russian as for English, and probably for all languages, and the psychological and physiological processes at work in the creations of the Russian Futurists, e.g. гопы-гопы, бра, жрт, ой, were possibly those operating at the dawn of language. If it is necessary to postulate origins for nonsense-words or nonce-words not derived from other words, some of the following theories may be found convincing: (1) that these words are imitations of other sounds (the 'Bow-wow' theory), (2) that they are expressions of pain or pleasure (the 'Pooh-pooh' theory), (3) that they are vocal reflexes set off by physical effort (the 'Yo-he-ho' theory), (4) that they are parts of rhythmic chanting or singing (the 'Sing-song' theory), (5) that the movements of the tongue and jaws and lips imitate those of other parts of the body (the 'Ta-ta' theory).[1] A less popular, but considerably older, theory maintains that words are in a mysterious harmony with the essential nature of the thing indicated.

Non-derived words may be meaningless (as are those quoted above) in that they do not symbolize anything, or they may be meaningful in that they denote a thing new to the speaker. The latter case is rare; it is very rarely necessary or convenient to attach a weird name to a newly invented, discovered or developed thing (although advertisers find this attention-arousing practice profitable). Children, coping with a universe of new objects and ideas, are the most fertile inventors of sound combinations. Both before and during the process of adaptation of his phonetic repertoire to the demands of the community in which he lives, the child emits sounds and combinations of sounds, first to express his feelings and later to name things. The order of appearance of phonemes is, as far as we can tell, surprisingly similar in most children, and it is probably due to physiological ease that children's names for near relations, for physical functions and for toys are similar in etymologically unrelated languages. Especially common in the language of young children (from about thirty-two weeks to three years old) are reduplicated syllables, most of which are meaningless to adults but some of which have become conventionalized as 'baby-talk' and have entered the language of grown-ups: e.g. *dada*, *mama*, *geegee* in English, тятя (father), ба́ба (old woman, grandmother), ца́ца (a toy) in Russian. This repetition of syllables in the language of children should not be confused with the reduplication practised by adults for specific semantic or stylistic ends (see §3F).

The creation of non-derived words by adults is very rare. Even more rarely do the exclamations or onomatopoeic groups that

[1] The names of these theories were invented by the American philologist, L. H. Gray.

make up the bulk of these words find their way into print. More deliberate creations, designed to produce striking (because unusual) phonetic effects, are found rarely in English (e.g. *quiz*, *Zixt*) and seemingly not at all in present-day Russian, although during the period of Futurism (*c.* 1913–25) an attempt was made (principally by Vyacheslav Ivanov, Khlebnikov and Kryuchonykh) to create a new language (за́умь) in which words would be evocative but not meaningful. None of these words (e.g. бра, ок, врзз) has survived in literary Russian and it is not possible in any case to arrange such words in grammatical classes.

Non-derived words are few in number and do not follow patterns which might serve as models for further creation: in no sense can the haphazard way in which they are made up be considered a regularly productive method of word formation.

3

DERIVATORY PROCEDURES: I

A. *Resemanticization*

Derivatory procedures not entailing formal change are little more systematic than non-derivatory methods. The distinction between meaning and form comes to mind when we are dealing with the procedures of *resemanticization* and *polysemanticization*. By these terms are meant respectively the replacement and the expansion of the meaning expressed by a given form. While it is undeniable that these processes are largely outside voluntary control and may be termed 'automatic' features of the historical development of languages, it is not unusual for new meanings deliberately to be given to words. The processes named above are different only in that in resemanticization the new meaning has quite ousted the old. The word мо́йка, originally 'the action of washing' (= мытьё) or 'place for washing clothes on a river bank', has reappeared in the modern мо́йка для посу́ды (a dish-washing machine). На́долбы, in the Middle Ages 'a palisade', in the nineteenth century 'palings', now means 'anti-tank defences'. In all cases of resemanticization a development of meaning may be traced (although sometimes with great difficulty, as in the case of the numeral and noun со́рок, at one time 'a number of furs', later 'forty furs' and now 'forty' or 'a group of forty churches'). It should be noted that resemanticization occurs in cases of change of grammatical class: the gerund зря (seeing) has disappeared, but the same form exists as an adverb with the meaning of 'in vain'. No nouns or adjectives are formed in this last way. Imperfectly understood or little-used borrowed words are especially subject to resemanticization: in Russian лилипу́т is now used to mean 'dwarf' and is used in its original meaning only in translations of Swift's novel.

Resemanticization is an infrequent phenomenon as it entails not only the extension but also the loss of meaning. It is to be expected that it is very rare except in nouns (and words based on nouns, e.g. лилипу́тский) as names of objects are often sufficiently imprecise to allow of their use over a long period of time, during which the objects themselves change. On the other hand, the qualities, actions, states or modes of action denoted by adjectives, verbs and adverbs (however imprecise these words may be) usually remain without change.

B. *Polysemanticization*

Polysemanticization is a widespread and continually operative process in all languages. It is the process seen in the accumulation of meanings expressible by English *joint* or *to hold*, or by Russian вту́лка (an insert) or стать (to become, stand up, begin). Replacement of meaning (see §3A) is rare, extension of meaning (of power to symbolize) is so common as to go unnoticed. The use of one form to denote an increasing number of ideas is perhaps the most intriguing of all the procedures of word formation because of the light it throws on the nature of meaning. To a large extent, the study of this procedure must be carried out on individual specimens: in the development of its meanings each word follows laws shaped by the oldest of these meanings. Yet a few general observations are valid and of direct relevance to the present study. In all Indo-European languages a difference in speed of semantic outgrowth may be seen in words of various grammatical categories. Nouns acquire new meanings through use in similes and metaphors and through readily made comparisons between old and new objects. The same noun may be used for a bull and for the tough support of a bridge (Rus. бык), or to denote a bubble, a blister, a kind of hot water bottle and a round, well-fed child (Rus. пузы́рь). The development of abstract from concrete meanings is common in nouns (Rus. пла́мя: 'flame; ardour, enthusiasm') and is of very frequent occurrence in adjectives (Rus. сла́дкий Eng. 'sweet', used of honey, tea, milk (= *fresh*), people (= *pleasant* or *hypocritical*), voices and smiles in both languages). Such extension of the meaning of adjectives has been largely a deliberate process in Russian due to the need for a very rapid enlargement of the vocabulary of the language which was first felt towards the end of the eighteenth century (see §6). The commonest Russian verbs, like those of English (*put*, *take*, *run*, *have*, *get*, *see*), have received some extension in meaning (e.g. смотре́ть is given in the Ushakov dictionary as a word of twelve distinct meanings), but it should not be forgotten that the meaning of these verbs is expressed in part by their predicates, and especially by the prepositions with which they are associated. Thus смотре́ть might be described as only part of a number of phrases distinct in meaning:

1. смотре́ть в (у́гол) (= to look at, into);
2. смотре́ть на (ребёнка) (= to look at);
3. смотре́ть (кни́гу) (= to become familiar with), смотре́ть (музе́й) (= to visit);
4. смотре́ть за (детьми́) (= to look after), etc.

The use of postpositions in English, which considerably reduces the apparently enormous number of meanings expressed by some verbs (*to get*, *to get at*, *to get by*, etc.), may be compared with the formally more striking use of verbal prefixes in Russian. The existence of such forms as рассмотре́ть (вопро́с) (to look into), пересмотре́ть (кни́гу) (to look over), etc., effectively relieves the unprefixed verb of possible semantic burdens and makes polysemanticization relatively unproductive in the Russian verb. It is, in fact, not to the verb, nor to the noun or adjective that we must turn to see the most impressive evidence of this procedure, but to the preposition. Here the development of meaning has been so profuse that it is impossible in some cases to give a concise definition to the functions of a preposition without resorting to etymological investigation. Russian по, for instance, is described by Ushakov as having thirty-five meanings. This luxuriant development is reflected to a considerable extent in the verbal prefixes of

Russian (which are prepositional/adverbial in origin) and thus in the nouns and adjectives derived from verbs (see §§8, 9). Purely nominal and adjectival prefixes are, however, far more limited in meaning.

Not all forms with multiple meanings are examples of polysemanticization. Rus. пробник may mean (1) 'a ram used for testing the readiness of ewes at mating time', (2) 'a testing device, probe'. The more specific meaning is the older. Here neither meaning has developed from the other. Instead, parallel development (affixation of -ник, in two of its functions, to the stem проб-) resulting in the creation of homophones has taken place. Only etymological investigation will distinguish beyond all doubt homophones such as these from forms which have undergone extension of meaning. As a rough guide, however, it can be said that polysemanticization is unlikely to have taken place if both the following conditions are fulfilled:

1. If the two meanings under comparison do not stand in a clear $A > B$ relationship.
2. If the word (or words) contains an affix of multiple meanings such as -ник, -щик.

C. *Conversion*

The use of a form in a new grammatical function (e.g. of the verb (*to*) *spy* as a noun (*a*) *spy*) is described by Jespersen (1922: 6.12) as 'one of the most characteristic traits of modern English'. This practice is, however, rare in Russian, almost certainly because of the importance of suffixes in distinguishing parts of speech.

A large number of adverbs and a smaller number of prepositions (e.g. босикóм, нóчью, ýжас; благодаря́, впереди́) are derived without change from other parts of speech, but this process does not play any part in the creation of nouns and adjectives in Russian.

D. *Internal modification*

In the words щекá/щёку and молод-óй/млáд-ший vowels or syllables within lexically identical roots differ. These alternations е/ё, оло/ла have no lexical or grammatical significance. This is true in modern Russian of nearly all alternations of vowels, whether of comparatively recent origin, as in the examples given above, or whether inherited from the Indo-European period. In the case of changes in the latter category it is important to bear in mind that vowel modification was originally a word-forming procedure and that in many languages (e.g. English) vowel-alternation is often lexically or grammatically significant. Only the vowel distinguishes English *seat* from *sit*. In the case of Russian гроб, грести́, however, the grammatical markers zero/-ti have completely usurped the original grammatical function of the internal vowels.

In the Slav languages vowel changes have served to distinguish the aspects of verbs (Rus. собира́ть/собра́ть; умира́ть/умере́ть) and to denote modes of action in verbs of motion (Rus. носи́ть/нести́) as well as to provide separate stems for nouns and verbs from the same root. This last function has become greatly obscured. The Russian verbal stems (при-)зыв(-а́ть), (при-)зв(-а́ть), (при-)зов(-ёт) are 'opposed' to the noun stems зов, (при-)зы́в. While in modern Russian the alternations are meaningful in a very few pairs of words (e.g. воз-и́-ла/вез-ла́), in the vast majority of cases they no longer carry grammatical or lexical meaning. For our purposes internal vowel changes are important only in that they may obscure the etymology of a noun or adjective and so impede comparisons. The Academy Grammar (§§ 167, 166) gives two useful lists of alternations, one of the vowel oppositions found in modern Russian and another of consonant changes which have arisen largely as a result of earlier changes in the vowel system. These consonant changes are of purely phonetic character and can in no case be considered meaningful.

E. *Accentual distinction*

Like vowel-alternation, a distinction in stress position is rarely meaningful in modern Russian except within the declension of nouns (e.g. реки́/ре́ки) and where it serves to separate one word from another (e.g. the adverb and gerund си́дя/сидя́). While English, with its lack of formal grammatical markers, has built up regular patterns of grammatically significant shifts (see Jespersen, 1922: 11.9), there are so few forms in Russian with ambiguous grammatical markers (including the 'zero suffix') that stress-alternation as a means of distinction is nearly always superfluous. As adverbs alone in modern Russian can be created from words of other grammatical categories without formal change, the use of stress-alternation cannot play any part in the formation of nouns or adjectives.

F. *Reduplication*

Reduplication (sometimes called 'gemination') is the repetition of a syllable or syllables with or without phonetic modification. Like vowel-alternation, it is a means of word formation which has become increasingly less common in the Indo-European languages. While Latin and Greek used partial reduplication to form verbal aspects, no such sophisticated uses are found for the procedure in either English or Russian. Reduplication in both languages is frequently the work of children, and such creations as English *dada* (giving *daddy*), *goody-goody* and Russian па́па, ца́ца (giving ца́цка) are not taken seriously by adults. Reduplication by adults is not uncommon but is usually a form of onomatopoeia (e.g. *clop-clop*): other forms are rarely literary. In Russian a few words of childish origin have been accepted into the written language (e.g. дя́дя, тётя, тя́тя, and several onomatopoeic verbs, e.g. гогота́ть, 'to cackle'). The syllables making up these words may be meaningful in themselves: this is true of the few 'intensive' adjectives formed by reduplication, e.g. круто́й-круто́й (extremely steep). Apart from the creation of childish nonce-words, onomatopoeic forms and an occasional adjective with intensified meaning, reduplication is not used to form nouns or adjectives in modern Russian.

4

DERIVATORY PROCEDURES: II

A. *Affixation and deaffixation. General*

Affixation (the addition of affixes to stems) and deaffixation (the dropping of affixes) are the two most important word-forming procedures in both English and Russian. These procedures can be applied widely and are therefore highly productive. To a limited extent the two procedures can be viewed in Russian as different dimensions of a single process, as the absence of affixes is as significant as their presence. In English, where the number of non-affixed ('base') stems is very large, the addition and subtraction of affixes are far more independent of one another than in Russian: as affixes rarely serve as markers of grammatical category, deaffixation before affixation is unusual in English. In Russian, however, affixes are frequently indispensable as grammatical markers and must be removed before the addition of fresh affixes. Only the stems of nouns, numerals and a few adjectives can exist without affixes (and therefore cannot undergo deaffixation).

Affixation is used in Russian in the derivation of both nouns and adjectives (as well as of words in other categories) from the stems of nouns, numerals, adjectives and verbs. Deaffixation without subsequent affixation is used only in the derivation of nouns.

The elements (morphemes) used in the two processes are called prefixes, infixes or suffixes, according to their position at the beginning, in the middle or towards the end of a word (i.e. before, within or after a root). Infixation is of great importance in the derivation of Russian verbs but plays no part in that of nouns or adjectives. In Russian, as in English, nominal and adjectival suffixes are far more numerous than nominal and adjectival prefixes. Although proportions vary from one language to another, this preponderance of suffixes is common to all Indo-European languages. Counting affixes used in the formation of nouns and adjectives (including deverbal nouns and adjectives) in the literary languages, we arrive at the following figures:

English: Prefixes 73; Suffixes 138;
Russian: Prefixes 78; Suffixes 204.

These figures do not take into account either formal varieties created by phonetic change or the multiple functions of any single form.

The similarity in the number of prefixes in English and Russian is largely accounted for by the prepositional origin of some two-thirds of these in each language. The etymology of the prefixes is much clearer than that of the suffixes and in some cases the English and Russian reflexions of a single Indo-European form are of similar meaning (e.g. for-/про-; on-/на-). Semantic stability of this order is not found in the suffixes and the original forms of these can be deduced only with difficulty because of the rapidity with which their forms change or are replaced.

Prefixes and suffixes contrasted

The meanings of prefixes in English and Russian are not only less susceptible to change than those of suffixes but also more powerful in relation to that of the stem. In any word containing both a prefix and a suffix the more radical change in meaning is effected by the removal of the prefix. Prefixes usually combine with stems to express new lexical meanings (e.g. Eng. press/depress/express/impress; Rus. ви́деть/зави́деть/ненави́деть/предви́деть). The addition of suffixes may bring about modification of the meaning of the stem but this never amounts to the loss of this meaning to any extent. The ideas expressed by the prefix-plus-stem in each of the above examples are preserved when suffixes are added as in English express/expression/expressive, and Russian предви́деть/предви́д-ен-ие/предви́д-енн-ый. Even where a stem is unprefixed a suffix cannot alter the meaning of the stem so far as to make us forget its meaning. Where the suffix has a considerable lexical content this is added to (not combined with) that of the stem, as in English actr-ess, occupi-er, bronch-itis; Russian актр-и́с-а, жил-е́ц, бронх-и́т. The most common functions of prefixes are adverbial and they can usually be replaced by an adverb or adverbial phrase (Rus. в-ход = движе́ние внутрь; анти-религио́зный = напра́вленный про́тив рели́гии). Prefixes of purely grammatical significance (as in с-де́лать, where с- expresses aspect) are found only in verbal and deverbal forms in Russian. In nouns and adjectives derived from these verbs the prefix either is meaningless (as in с-де́л-к-а, 'a deal') or preserves the notion of perfectivity (as in с-де́ль-н-ая рабо́та, 'piece-work', i.e. 'completed' work). Apart from such rare exceptions, all prefixes are lexically meaningful. There are no prefixes of emotive meaning which may be compared to the diminutive and augmentative suffixes (see §9).

In contrast to prefixes, suffixes often express a wide and diffuse range of lexical meanings and are frequently of purely grammatical significance. The most common noun and adjective suffixes in Russian (-ен-ие, -ость; -н-, -ов-, -ск-) are used to denote relationship. This may be semantic as in изумл-е́н-ие, 'the condition resultant from *X*', where изуми́ть is 'the performance of *X*'; or grammatical (the expression of place in one of the grammatical categories or of relationship to the rest of the sentence) as in the same example, изумл-éн-ие, in which the suffix indicates that this is a noun. The addition of the suffix -ен-ие by a native speaker defines the meaning of the stem (and prefix) both lexically and grammatically.

The suffixes, not only of Russian, but of all the Indo-European languages, were for the most part originally lexical rather than grammatical. Over the whole range of suffixes this lexical content has been preserved to a far lesser extent than in prefixes. There are purely grammatical suffixes (e.g. English *-al*, Russian -н- in adjectives) and almost purely lexical suffixes (e.g. English *-arian*, Russian -ник), but in nearly all cases both types of function (relating and denoting) are present. Compare the relationships between the two roots in the following Russian phrases and notice how difficult it is to separate the grammatical and lexical functions of the suffixes used. Notice also how some purely grammatical meanings (number, case) are expressed not by suffixes but by terminations.

1. тёпл-ый луч (a warm ray).
2. тепл-от-á луч-á (the warmth of the ray).
3. луч-и́ст-ая тепл-от-á (radiant heat).
4. из-лучéн-ие тепл-от-ы́ (the radiation of heat).
1*a*. тёпл-ые луч-и́ (warm rays).
2*a*. тепл-от-á луч-éй (the warmth of the rays).

Affixes used in Russian nouns and adjectives may be grouped as follows:

Prefixes proper to nouns and adjectives alone (53).
Prefixes used in deverbal nouns and adjectives (25).
Noun suffixes (145).
Adjective suffixes (59).

In the account of the functions of affixes which follows the last two groups are dealt with together to aid comparison.

B. *Prefixes*

(1) *Prefixes proper to non-deverbal nouns and adjectives*

Not all prefixed nouns and adjectives are deverbal. It is possible to derive nouns from other nouns and adjectives from other adjectives by prefixation alone (e.g. архи-ерéй, 'an archbishop', супер-облóжка, 'a dustcover'; анти-религиóзный, 'anti-religious', наи-лу́чший, 'best'), and both nouns and adjectives from nouns by simultaneous prefixation and suffixation (e.g. бес-плóд-ие, 'infertility', вз-мóр-ье, 'a coast'; под-зéм-н-ый, 'underground', сверх-мéр-н-ый, 'excessive'). Where a prefixed and unprefixed adjective have both been derived from a noun, as is the case with сверхмéр-н-ый and мéр-н-ый (measured), simultaneous prefixation and suffixation can be distinguished only by an appeal to meaning. Here the addition of сверх- to the latter adjectival form would produce a new adjective *сверх-мерный with a meaning equivalent to the English 'super-measured'. Unless we accept that the addition of a prefix can affect the function of a suffix (for the functions of -н- in мéрный and сверхмéрный differ considerably) it appears reasonable to regard сверхмéрный as formed from the noun мéра *by analogy with* one of the phrases сверх мéры/сверх мер. A phrase of similar structure (preposition + noun in an oblique case) and of closely comparable meaning exists alongside most prefixed and suffixed nouns and adjectives (e.g. без плодá, под землёй, сверх мéры), and the attempted construction of such a phrase helps in the translation of these words. It seems unlikely, however, that phrases of the type без плодá act as *underlays* to the derived words, as do the phrases represented by abbreviated compounds (see pp. 48–51), in view of the existence of prefixed and suffixed nouns and adjectives to which no phrases correspond (e.g. вз-мóр-ье, зá-мороз-к-и, 'light frost').

Prefixed non-deverbal nouns may be formed from other nouns or from adjectives. Prefixed non-deverbal adjectives may be formed from other adjectives or from nouns. Prefixed nouns may be derived from non-prefixed nouns with or without simultaneous suffixation, as in из-голóв-ье (the head of a bed), зá-мороз-к-и, архи-ерéй, со-áвтор (a co-author). Derivation from nouns already prefixed as in супер-облóжка is rare and is never accompanied by suffixation.

Prefixed nouns are most commonly derived from prefixed adjectives by the addition of a suffix (usually -н-ость, -ник or -ниц-а) as in а-морáль-н-ость (amorality), до-шкóль-ниц-а (a girl of pre-school age). The popularity of the suffixes quoted is probably due to the frequency with which н appears in the prefixed adjectives of origin (here аморáль-н-ый, дошкóль-н-ый).

There appear to be no cases of derivation of prefixed nouns from unprefixed adjectives or adjective stems which might be compared to the creation of adjectives from unprefixed nouns by simultaneous prefixation and suffixation (e.g. of по-смéрт-н-ый, 'posthumous', from смерть). Prefixed adjectives may also be derived from unprefixed adjectives (e.g. пре-дóбрый, 'very kind, very good') and from adjectives already prefixed (e.g. невосприи́мчивый, 'unreceptive'). In neither instance is suffixation required.

Prefixation is used in five ways to derive nouns or adjectives from other nouns and adjectives:

1. Prefixation to form nouns from other nouns without simultaneous suffixation, as in со-áвтор, супер-облóжка.

2. Prefixation to form adjectives from other adjectives, as in а-морáльный, пре-дóбрый.

3. Prefixation to form adjectives from nouns with the addition of a grammatical termination only, as in без-волóсый, 'hair-less'.

4. Prefixation to form nouns from other nouns with simultaneous suffixation, as in из-голóв-ье, зá-мороз-к-и.

5. Prefixation to form adjectives from nouns with simultaneous suffixation as in по-смéрт-н-ый, под-москóв-н-ый, 'near Moscow'.

Broadly speaking, two sets of forms may be distinguished. The prefixes which may be used without accompanying suffixation (а-, анти-, архи-, без-, все-, интер-, наи-, не-, про-, псевдо-, раз-, сверх-, со-, су-, суб-, супер-, транс-, экс-, etc.) are not, apart from раз- and со-, used in the formation of verbs. Пре- and про- are here of different meaning to the verbal prefixes of the same form. Без- and the recently borrowed prefixes are used in verbs only when they are derived from nouns that are already prefixed (e.g. бездéйствовать, 'to be inactive', from бездéйствие, 'inactivity').

Prefixes which may be used together with suffixes (без-, вз-, вне-, внутри-, до-, за-, между-/меж-, на-, над-, о-, от-, по-, под-, пред-, прежде-, при-, противо-, сверх-, среди-, etc.) are for the most part to be found in non-denominal verbs as well as in nouns and adjectives. Exceptions are the relatively little-used prefixes без-, вне-, внутри-, между-, прежде-, противо-, сверх-, and среди-.

For the most part the prefixes of the second group present remarkable similarities in meaning to the verbal prefixes with which they form homonyms, but one important difference in function must be noted. In these prefixes, as in those of the first group, no trace is to be found of the grammatical functions associated with verbal prefixes. This is to say that prefixes proper to nouns and adjectives exert a purely lexical influence on the stems to which they are joined and that the functions of these prefixes are far more limited and more easily defined than those of the prefixes used with verbal stems.

Of the fifty-three prefixes (including the compound prefix не-без-) used in non-deverbal nouns and adjectives nearly all present a single lexical meaning (e.g. архи- means only 'intensely', на- means only 'on top of', пред- means only 'immediately before'): exceptions are по- and под- (see §§8, 9). When compared with the verbal prefixes with which they share a common etymology, prefixes of the second group present little refinement of meaning. This is possibly because of a close similarity in function with prepositions of which they reflect only the more concrete meanings.

Simultaneous suffixation is performed for purely grammatical ends in the derivation of adjectives from unprefixed nouns. The suffixes -н-, -ск- and, rarely, -ов- are used, none of these having a lexical content. The suffixes which may be added in the derivation of nouns from other nouns are, however, lexically meaningful. Nouns formed by the addition of the prefix без- and the suffix -ие/-ье denote a condition from which the noun of origin is absent, as in без-закóн-ие (lawlessness), бес-плóд-ие (infertility) (= absence of закóн, плод). The same suffix is used in association with the spatial prefixes вз-, за-, по-, под-, пре-, при- to form nouns denoting relatively large and poorly defined places, as in вз-мóр-ье (seaside), За-байкáл-ье (the area east of Lake Baikal), при-озéр-ье (the land near a lake). The prefix со- is used with -ие/-ье to denote coincidence or agglomeration, as in со-звéзд-ие (a constellation), со-звýч-ие (harmony). The prefixes на-, над-, о-, под-, пред- are used with the suffix -ник to form nouns denoting objects named according to their spatial relationship with other objects, e.g. на-ýш-ник-и (earphones), под-окóн-ник (a window-sill).

In denominal nouns with simultaneous prefixation and suffixation the noun of origin may preserve its form (as in без-закóн-ие) if masculine, but is normally replaced by the stem (as in со-звéзд-ие, без-врéмен-ье, 'a time of inaction') if feminine or neuter.

All the prefixes are listed, with examples of nouns and adjectives, in §9.

(2) *Prefixes in deverbal nouns and adjectives*

Nouns may be derived from verbs by desuffixation (as in топь, 'a marsh', прóрезь, 'a slit', ухóд, 'departure') or by resuffixation (as in стрел-óк, 'a rifleman', возрожд-éн-ие, 'Renascence'). Adjectives may be derived from verbs by resuffixation only (as in желá-тель-н-ый, 'desirable', подвиж-н-óй, 'mobile'). In all cases any prefix found in the verb of origin is preserved (as here in прó-резь, у-хóд, воз-рождéние, по-движнóй from прорéза́ть, уходи́ть, возроди́ть, подви́га́ть).

While the form of the prefix remains intact in deverbal nouns and adjectives the range of its functions is considerably narrowed. Verbal prefixes have two possible grammatical functions, the expression of perfectivity and the expression of a change in transitiveness/intransitiveness. The first and more common of these functions applies *only* to verbs and is reflected only in participial adjectives (e.g. обдýманный план, 'a well-thought-out plan') derived from perfective verbs. The lexical (= modal) meanings frequently accompanying perfectivity (completion, thoroughness) may, however, be detected in the prefixes of some deverbal nouns and adjectives (e.g. с-дéлка, 'a deal', с-дéльная рабóта, 'piece-work'). The second function, which may be equated with the expression of transitiveness as in обходи́ть (to avoid, overtake) (compare ходи́ть), may be seen in a few deverbal nouns and adjectives (e.g. об-хóд болóта, закóна, 'avoidance of a bog, the law'; об-хóдный манёвр, 'a flanking movement'). In some cases this meaning is not apparent, as in об-хóдный путь (a roundabout way), where no object is clearly implied and the prefix may well have none but lexical (adverbial, prepositional) meaning.

The lexical functions of verbal prefixes may be generally described as adverbial. The prefixes indicate the direction or manner (mode) in which an act is performed or the duration of a state. Most prefixed verbs (e.g. положи́ть, 'to lay') are susceptible to metaphorical use. The prefixes are with very few exceptions etymologically identical with prepositions at present in use, and the meanings of prefixes and prepositions with similar forms (e.g. до-, из-, от-) coincide to varying extents. In all cases, however, the verbal prefix has developed modal meanings not found in the corresponding preposition, which expresses only spatial, temporal and telic relationships between persons and things. These modal meanings are also adverbial, being indications of the nature of an act or state with regard to (*a*) its course of development (inchoative, ingressive, momentary), (*b*) its intensity (superficial, intensive) and (*c*) the number of subjects or objects with which it has to do (distributive, non-distributive). Further modal meanings qualifying that of the stem may be expressed by infixes.

Only certain members of most groups of verbal homonyms yield nouns and adjectives. Thus it is possible to derive a noun покры́тие from only six of the eleven homonyms покры́ть. Where derivation is possible, however, the lexical meanings of the verbal prefix are well preserved and no new meanings are found in the prefix of the derived noun or adjective. The form покры́ть may be said to express any of eleven lexical meanings (or to be appropriate in any of eleven types of context) and the form покры́тие may be said to express any of six meanings all of which are included in the eleven mentioned above.

Not all verbs generate nouns and adjectives. Derivation from reflexive forms is rare and many uncommon verbs (e.g. загры́зть, 'to gnaw to death') yield no derived words except passive participles which may be used as adjectives. Further, of the whole range of verbs with any prefix only those with certain essential meanings are able to generate nouns and adjectives. For example, verbs with the prefix на- may express any of the following ideas: (1) movement upon a surface or on to an object, as in набро́сить, напластова́ть, наскочи́ть; (2) accumulation of subjects or objects, as in набежа́ть (набежа́ло мно́го наро́ду, 'a lot of people rushed up'), накопи́ть, нарасти́; (3) intensity, as in наговори́ть, наклевета́ть, напи́ться; (4) superficiality, as in напева́ть, насви́стывать. Nouns and adjectives may be derived only from verbs in the first two categories.

Deverbal prefixed nouns may be recognized by formal features. While a few nouns are created from prefixed verbs by deaffixation the majority are formed by the replacement of the suffix/termination of the infinitive by a noun suffix. Of the twenty-three suffixes used with prefixed verbal stems only about a half are common. These are -ие, -ен-ие, -н-ие, -к-а, -ник, -м-ость, -н-ость, -тель, -щик/-чик as in закры́т-ие (closing), изобрет-е́н-ие (an invention), замеча́-н-ие (a remark), попра́в-к-а (correction, a correction), подъём-ник (a lift), вмести́-м-ость (capacity), влюбл-ённ-ость (infatuation), выключа́-тель (a switch), покуп-щи́к (a purchaser), растра́т-чик (an embezzler), счёт-чик (a meter).

Deverbal prefixed adjectives cannot be distinguished from those of non-verbal origin unless their stems are recognized.

C. *Noun and adjective suffixes*

Suffixes are used to form nouns and adjectives from the stems of nouns (as in кавка́з-ец, 'a Caucasian'; бород-а́т-ый, 'bearded'), adjectives (мал-ы́ш, 'a small child'; горьк-ов-а́т-ый, 'rather bitter'), verbs (рабо́т-ник, 'a worker'; пуг-ли́в-ый, 'timid') and numerals (пе́рв-ен-ств-о, 'supremacy, championship'; двой-ств-енн-ый, 'dual'). Nouns may be derived by suffixation from the stems of participles (ста́вл-ен-ник, 'a figurehead, puppet'). Adjectives may be derived in this way from the stems of adverbs (вчера́-ш-н-ий, 'yesterday's').

The forms used in this important procedure are numerous. Ignoring homonyms there are 145 noun suffixes and 59 adjective suffixes. No two of these are identical in grammatical function, lexical function, applicability and productiveness, although very close similarities exist between the members of some pairs of adjectival suffixes (e.g. -н-, -ск-). Less than half of these suffixes (43 noun, 21 adjective) are described as productive or very productive in the Academy Grammar. Forty-three noun and 12 adjective suffixes are weakly productive (usually through restricted applicability), 57 noun and 18 adjective suffixes are completely unproductive and to this group must be added 2 noun and 8 adjective suffixes that are probably unperceived and so 'isolatable' only. The use of the productive and very productive suffixes is illustrated in §8, while suffixes of all degrees of productiveness are listed in §9.

There are several notable differences between noun and adjective suffixes. In the nominative singular noun suffixes may take a gender termination but not a case ending. Adjective suffixes are nearly all followed by the endings -ый, -ая, -ое (etc.), exceptions being the possessives -ин/-ын, -нин, -ов.

Compound suffixes are more numerous and more common in adjectives, which are often derived from suffixed nouns (e.g. кладби́щ-ен-ск-ий, 'cemetery'). Nouns are less commonly formed from suffixed adjectives and a compound noun suffix normally denotes a feminine equivalent of the word expressed by the noun with a single suffix (e.g. говор-у́н-ья, 'a talkative woman'). But a note of caution is due as -анец, -ианец, -анка, -ианка may be considered compound suffixes.

The applicability and therefore the frequency of occurrence of suffixes are determined by three factors: the lexical content of the suffix, the category of stem (noun, verb, etc.) to which it may be joined and the nature of the phonetic contexts in which it may be used. These factors restrict the use of every noun and adjective suffix: not even the suffixes of very general (i.e. grammatical) meaning may be attached to any kind of stem irrespective of the phonetic conditions at the end of that stem. In general, however, an adjective suffix is more widely used and may be expected to be more common than a noun suffix. Lexical meaning is absent from, or very restricted in, many adjective suffixes (e.g. -н-, -ов-, -ск-), a phenomenon rare in noun suffixes, which usually denote *either* persons *or* objects *or* abstractions. Only in a handful of cases (e.g. -ец, as in варен-е́ц, 'fermented milk', румя́н-ец, 'a blush, glow', сам-е́ц, 'a male') is it impossible to ascribe to the suffix a (small) number of clearly definable lexical meanings.

Noun suffixes are attached to a wider variety of stems than are adjective suffixes. Nouns are almost as frequently derived from adjectives as from other nouns or from verbs: 25 per cent of noun suffixes are attached to adjective stems, 40 per cent to noun stems, 31 per cent to verb stems, and a handful to the stems of participles and numerals. Adjectives, however, are comparatively rarely formed from other adjectives: 64 per cent of adjective suffixes are attached to noun stems, 24 per cent to verb stems and only 8 per cent to adjective stems.

Adjectives are absolutely more numerous than nouns but there is a greater number of noun suffixes, probably because of the two factors already mentioned. The tendency to use different suffixes with stems of different categories multiplies the variety of noun suffixes created by lexical specialization. Phonetic limitations appear to affect the use of both noun and adjective suffixes equally slightly.

In few cases are the lexical functions of suffixes identical but the very great degree of correspondence between the functions of certain suffixes (e.g. the noun suffixes -ник, -щик, the adjectival suffixes -л-яв-, -ч-ат-) enables us to speak of lexical functions common to a group of suffixes. Grammatical functions (the expression of substance, quality, relationship, etc.) are few in number, easily distinguished and each common to a large number of forms.

Of the lexical functions of the noun suffixes the following are the most common. The suffixes are used to form nouns denoting:

1. Objects (e.g. двйга-тель, 'a motor'; лйств-ен-ниц-а, 'a larch'; вéша-л-к-а, 'a hook, hanger'; грáдус-ник, 'a thermometer').

2. Abstractions (e.g. глýп-ость, 'stupidity'; равнодýш-ие, 'equanimity'; достóин-ств-о, 'value, worth'; тур-йзм, 'tourism, touring').

3. Male persons (e.g. вýз-ов-ец, 'a university student'; америк-áн-ец, 'an American'; зуб-н-йк, 'a dentist'; застýп-ник, 'an intercessor'; барабáн-щик, 'a drummer').

4. Female persons (e.g. крестья-н-к-а, 'a peasant woman'; стар-ýх-а, 'an old woman'; францýж-ен-к-а, 'a Frenchwoman'; безбóж-ниц-а, 'an atheist').

5. Persons of either sex (e.g. бедн-яг-а, 'a poor person'; вы́скоч-к-а, 'an upstart'; плáк-с-а, 'a cry-baby'; опив-óх-а, 'an habitual drunkard').

A few noun suffixes are found in words denoting mature animals (e.g. коз-ёл, 'a he-goat', сам-éц) and the young of animals (e.g. козл-ён-ок, 'a kid') and a considerable number are used in diminutive and augmentative forms. The grammatical function of the noun suffixes (the creation of names for things, ideas, people and animals according to their qualities or their associations with other objects) calls for no comment.

The majority of adjectival suffixes have no lexical functions and serve only to denote that the words of which they are part are possessive, or relative/undifferentiated (qualitative) adjectives (e.g. брáт-н-ин, 'brother's', брáт-ск-ий, 'fraternal'). Lexicality is involved only in those cases in which the suffix has a modal or emotive meaning, that is, where it indicates the degree to which a quality is exhibited or the attitude of the speaker or writer to the existence of the quality, as in бел-ов-áт-ый (whitish), дыр-яв-ый (full of holes), уш-áст-ый (having (disagreeably) large ears). All of the suffixes (8 per cent of the total) used with adjective stems present one or both of these types of lexical meaning.

In general it may be said that the functions of noun suffixes are predominantly lexical while those of adjective suffixes are predominantly grammatical. For practical purposes this contrast means that the student may translate words with adjective suffixes, and compose words, using these suffixes, with a degree of freedom impermissible in his dealings with noun suffixes. The functions of the suffixes most useful to the student are illustrated in §8.

D. *Functions of deaffixation*

Two types of deaffixation may be distinguished by their functions: preparatory and complete deaffixation. *Complete deaffixation* is the dropping of affixes and terminations to leave bared stems, as in новь (virgin soil) formed from нóвый. *Preparatory deaffixation* is the dropping of affixes which takes place before the addition of alternative affixes. It is the first stage in the replacement of prefixes and suffixes, as seen in америк-áн-ец, америк-áн-к-а, америк-áн-ский. Preparatory deaffixation leaves no formal traces and its operation must be deduced, but this can only be done with absolute certainty when, as in the example given, the affixed stem does not exist bare. For this reason, and because preparatory deaffixation presents no lexical or grammatical functions of interest to the learner, there is little point in discussing it further.

Complete deaffixation may also be called *complete desuffixation* as only final elements are lost in this process, which is used in the derivation of nouns from verbs, adjectives and other nouns, and of the 'units of composition' (see below) from verbs. The procedure may be regarded as largely fulfilling the same lexico-grammatical functions as its formal opposite, suffixation: words belonging to one grammatical category are derived from those of another or, less commonly, from words of the same category, the root meaning of the original and derived words being identical. The similarity in the functions of the two procedures may be readily appreciated by comparing examples of derived words.

Suffixation produces nouns from unprefixed verbs such as ходь-б-á (walking), ход-óк (a walker), from ходи́ть; nouns from prefixed verbs such as возрожд-éн-ие (Renascence), from возрождáть; nouns from adjectives such as свéж-есть (freshness), from свéжий; and nouns from other nouns such as комсомóл-ец (a Komsomol member), from комсомóл. Deaffixation also produces nouns from unprefixed verbs, such as цветы́ (flowers), from цвести́ (to bloom); nouns from prefixed verbs, such as прохóд (a passage), from проходи́ть; nouns from adjectives, such as чернь (niello), from чёрный; and nouns from other nouns, such as доя́р (a milking-machine operator), from доя́рка (a milkmaid). In addition to these shared functions, suffixation is used to make adjectives (and adverbs and verbs) from nouns, verbs, adjectives, and, rarely, from other parts of speech. Deaffixation too has a peculiar function, the creation of *units of composition* from verbs. These elements are used in compounds after the loss of the infinitive termination and the verbal suffix (-е-, -а-, -ну-, etc.) and function as nouns. They are nearly all taken from unprefixed imperfective verbs, e.g. -вод from водить, -нос from носить, -руб from рубить, as in пчеловод (a beekeeper), водонос (a water-carrier), лесоруб (a forester). While a few units of composition are created from prefixed verbs, e.g. -провод, from проводить, as in нефтепровод (an oil pipe-line), the desuffixation of these verbs normally produces nouns. The prefixed verbs of motion (imperfective aspect) are very prolific in this respect, compounds of ходить alone yielding twenty nouns such as подход (an approach), проход, уход (departure).

The creation of units of composition and of nouns from verbs is the most common lexico-grammatical function of deaffixation, the formation of new nouns from adjectives in this way being practically unknown in most literary styles. It should be noted, however, that a number of twentieth-century poets (Blok, Bal'mont, Yesenin, Kogan, Mayakovsky, Khlebnikov) show a predilection for *ad hoc* creations by deaffixation. The invented forms водь, гладь, загробь, нищь, толщь, ясь (Mayakovsky), are readily understood upon comparison with the adjectives from which they are derived. Nouns formed from other nouns by the loss of a gender ending, e.g. берёзь (a group of birch trees), appear to be used only by Yesenin.

(On *units of composition* see also §§5B, 5C, pp. 44–7.)

E. *Phonetic effects of affixation and deaffixation*

When affixes are attached to or detached from stems, phonetic changes may take place in these stems at the point of junction. For instance, the stem (final stem) consonants г, к, х are replaced by ж, ч, ш when the suffix -ье is added to the stem, as in побереж-ье (a littoral). The stem consonants б, в, м are replaced by бл, вл, мл before the suffix -ан-ин/-ян-ин, as in римл-ян-ин (a Roman). All stem consonants with soft counterparts are replaced by these counterparts when the adjective suffix -янн- is added to the stem, as in стекл-янн-ый (glass), cf. стекл-о. The same process usually takes place in adjective stems bared by the loss of suffix or termination, e.g. in новь (virgin soil).

In prefixation the prefix is more often modified than the stem, either by a loss of sonority, as in рас-скáз (a story), ис-хóдный (initial) (cf. раз-говóр, 'a conversation', из-бежáние, 'avoidance'), or by the addition of a vowel, either medially, as in вос-тóк (east), or finally, as in во-прóс (a question) (cf. вс-потéлый, 'sweating'; в-ложéние, 'insertion'). Only stems beginning with the vowel и are modified, and then not after all prefixes. Of the prefixes found in nouns and adjectives those with forms in -о, e.g. во-, взо-, usually cause the replacement of и by й as in про-йдóха (a shrewd man). Where there is immediate contact between the hard consonant of a prefix and the initial и of a stem, the latter is replaced by ы as in без-ымя́нный (nameless), с-ыск (a police investigation). In the same phonetic context the other front vowels are unchanged, and no softening of the prefix consonant takes place. This lack of interaction is shown orthographically by a hard sign, as in предъявлéние и́ска (the bringing of an action).

The insertion of an -н- between the prefixes в-, с- and the initial vowel of a stem, as in вн-имáние (attention) and сн-ятóе молокó (skimmed milk), is very rare and may be ignored for practical purposes.

Noun and adjective suffixes, as indicated above, vary widely in their power to cause phonetic change. The addition of a suffix may bring about any of three phonetic changes (softening, palatalization, mutation), or no change, in the final consonant of the stem.

First, and most commonly, *softening* may take place. All suffixes beginning with the letters я, е, и, ё, ю (whether or not they may be written at other times with initial а, ы, о or у) permit the preceding stem-consonant to retain its softness, as in дел-éн-ие (division) from дел-и́-ть, or cause it to become soft, as in коз-ёл from козá, unless this is impossible due to the lack of an appropriate counterpart, as in свéж-есть (freshness) from свéжий, or unless a more severe change (mutation) takes place. Softening may be caused by suffixes beginning with a soft sign (e.g. -ье) or with a soft or historically soft consonant (e.g. -чин-а, -ш-а) or with a consonant which was earlier preceded by a soft sign representing a reduced front vowel (e.g. -б-а < -ьб-а, -ник < -ьник). In the last two cases softening may occur only sporadically. It is often not represented in spelling: the consonant preceding the suffix in отшéль-ник (a hermit), рабóт-ник (a workman), подокóн-ник (a window-sill), are all soft. There appears to be no correlation between softening and lexical function, and the only phonetic 'rule' that can be given is that the sound л is frequently replaced by ль. The suffixes causing changes of this kind are: -б-а, -н-, -ник, -ниц-а, -ни-ч-еств-о, -ск-, -ств-о, -ша, -щик/-чик, -щин-а/-чин-а, -щиц-а/-чиц-а.

Secondly, a suffix may cause the replacement of some or all of the labial consonants б, п, в, ф, м, when these are final in stems, by the double sounds spelt as бл, пл, вл, фл, мл. This change is the result of a high degree of softening (sometimes called *palatalization*) and operates under the conditions specified for the first change. Alternation of soft and very soft labials is common in forms of verbal origin, e.g. влюби́ться (to fall in love), влюбл-ённ-ость (being in love).

Thirdly, the stem-consonant may be not merely softened or palatalized but replaced by a quite different sound. This change (*mutation*) reflects no alteration in meaning, occurs before only twenty or so of the noun and adjective suffixes and concerns only eight stem-consonants (д, т; к, г, х; ц, з, с). Nevertheless, mutation is of greater importance to the student than either degree of softening. The patterns of mutation are easy to memorize, but failure to do so will hinder the recognition of stems and lead to the setting up of bad habits in active word building.

Four sets of mutations occur, all due to phonetic influences that are no longer obvious.

1. The stem-consonants -к, -г, -х are replaced by -ч, -ж, -ш when any of the following suffixes is added to the stem:

-ан-/-ян-, -ар/-яр, -ат-, -ен-ие/-н-ие, -ен-к-а, -енн-, -ённ-, -еств-о, -ин-к-а, -их-а, -лив-, -ник, -ниц-а, -ск-/-еск-, -ь-, -ье, -ьё.

2. The stem-consonants -ц, -з are replaced by -ч, -ж when any of the following suffixes is added to the stem:

-еск-, -еств-, -ник (ц/ч only).

3. The stem-consonant д may be replaced by either ж or жд, т is replaced by щ and the clusters ск, ст are also replaced by щ when the suffixes -ан-/-ян-, -ен-ие, -енн-, -ённ-, are added.

4. The stem-consonant с is replaced by ш before both the suffixes listed under (3) and the suffix -ь-.

The operation of mutation before these suffixes is illustrated in §8.

The phonetic effects of (complete) deaffixation are of less practical importance to the student than are those of affixation.

Mutation is very rare, being now confined to nouns derived from adjective stems in -к, -г, -х, e.g. тишь (silence). Softening takes place in deadjectival nouns, as in высь (a height), зе́лень (greenery): contrast ухо́д (departure), from the verb уходи́ть. In the last example hardening, customary in nouns derived from verb stems ending in a soft consonant, has taken place. Softening or mutation may, however, be observed in a few deverbal nouns of great age, e.g. тварь (a creature), вождь (a leader), originally from the Old Church Slavonic verbs творити, водити. A consequence of deaffixation that is seen only in words inherited from Old Church Slavonic is the addition of gender endings to nouns derived both from verbs and from adjectives, as in похвала́ (praise) (from похвалити), and зло (evil) (from зълыи).

F. *The etymology of affixes*

The number of affixes in all languages varies with the passage of time as does the size of the lexicon. In Russian, as in all languages using these elements, (1) some affixes have ceased to be perceived as such, e.g. -р in дар (a gift), пир (a feast), (2) some have been replaced by others of identical function and similar applicability, e.g. no new nouns are formed with -ух, -ч as in пету́х (a cock), ткач (a weaver), while (3) others have been imported into the language from other languages, e.g. -ист as in тури́ст, or from dialects and uneducated speech, e.g. -ущ- as in толсту́щий (very fat), or (4) have been created from morphemes already existing in the language, e.g. -ов-ск- as in шекспи́ровский (Shakespearian). But despite numerous additions and losses, the list of most commonly used affixes remained the same in essence throughout the history of the written language until about 250 years ago. The period since the time of Peter the Great has seen remarkable changes in the relative popularity of native (Slavonic) and imported (French, English, 'International') affixes. Foreign prefixes, now nearly as numerous as those of native origin, are used with a high degree of productiveness (on productiveness see §4G) in the formation of nouns and adjectives, and in some cases have replaced native prefixes with similar functions. The nineteenth-century creations противонаро́дный, противомонархи́ческий, have disappeared, their places being taken by антинаро́дный and антимонархи́ческий. Dal's dictionary (1881) lists three words with the prefix интер-: the Orthographical Dictionary (1956) lists thirty-six nouns and adjectives alone with this prefix.

Changes in the relative popularity of native and imported suffixes are equally remarkable. As in the case of prefixes, a certain number of foreign elements may be discounted as unperceived and so non-productive, but of those remaining eight foreign noun suffixes (those in words such as пилот-áж, курс-áнт, агит-áц-ия, субъектив-и́зм, большев-и́ст, агит-áт-ор, кандидат-у́р-а and электр-и-фик-áц-ия) are productive (P), a further four are weakly productive (WP) and five more are non-productive (NP). The noun suffixes of Slavonic origin are far more numerous (114), but 40 per cent of these are completely unproductive and a further 28 per cent are only weakly productive.

Foreign elements are equally prominent but less important among the adjective suffixes. While one adjective suffix in five (11 out of 58) is imported, native suffixes are vastly more productive. Moreover, every one of the foreign affixes is followed by a native element, as in интеллект-уáль-*н*-ый and англ-и́й-*ск*-ий, and, perhaps as a consequence, all but one (-ий-, < -ия) are unperceived and quite unproductive.

It is usually difficult to trace the origin of the foreign noun and adjective prefixes and suffixes. In many cases the immediate source of a word containing a foreign element is known, but the presence of the same element in other languages, allowing for adaptation to the phonetic norms of each language, prevents our regarding the first language as the source of all words containing that element. The word комфорт-áбель-н-ый is a Russian version of the English word 'comfortable', first recorded in 1837, but -абель-н- may not be regarded as a suffix 'of English origin' as it is also found in words that are Russian versions of French adjectives in *-able* (e.g. резонáбельный) and German adjectives in *-abel*. In this case it is least misleading to call the origin of the affix 'French and International', because most words in which it occurs (including the oldest, нерезонáбельный, 1717) are taken immediately from French. The term *International* denotes the wide currency of the affix in the languages of the Greco-Roman or 'western' cultures. It is the increasing use of International affixes and stems that has led during the last two centuries to a remarkable growing together of the technical vocabularies of many languages, including English and Russian. This standardization of lexicon is also found, to a more limited extent, in the non-specialized literary languages. The naming of emotions, ideas and newly invented objects has been performed in many languages with extensive use of common affixes and stems. In every case these forms can be traced back to Latin (including medieval Latin) and often to Greek. The example quoted (-абель-) originated as the Latin suffix *-abilis* but was not used with the stem seen in Russian as комфорт- until the two were brought together in Old French.

Affixes of foreign origin are assimilated into Russian to different degrees. Full acceptance is marked by the use of such an affix with a native root; thus -ист, used with imported stems throughout the eighteenth century, may be said to have become a 'Russian' suffix not much before 1825, when the word гусли́ст (a psaltery player) was first recorded. Where foreign affixes are not used with native roots it is doubtful whether the former are perceived as affixes by Russian speakers. Where a foreign root is found with one or more of these affixes or both with the affix and with no affix, as in ве́на (a vein), вено́зный (venous), the affix can be isolated, but this is no guarantee that it is recognized as an affix by Russian speakers and that it therefore has a potential word-building function. Imported affixes which are unproductive and which may not be perceived by speakers of Russian are marked (*Isol. only*) in §9.

All the verbal prefixes, just over half of the prefixes proper to nouns and adjectives, 85 per cent of the noun suffixes and 79 per cent of the adjective suffixes in Russian are, however, of native origin. 'Native origin' means that, as far as we can tell, these affixes have been used by speakers of Russian since pre-literary times.

The native affixes have various sources. Only in the case of prefixes have satisfactory etymologies been established, and even here there are gaps and points of disagreement. In nearly all cases, however, the origin of a prefix is also that of the preposition formally most similar to it, and these common etymologies throw much light on the semantic development of the prefixes в-, до-, за-, из-, на-, над-, о/об-, от-, по-, под-, пред-, при-, про-, с- and у-. All of these (except for за-) and the remaining prefixes (вз-, вы-, низ-, пере-, пре-, раз-) of native origin can be traced back to supposed Indo-European forms and so related to prefixes and prepositions in other languages. Etymological investigation shows, for instance, that Russian вы- and English *out-* have developed from the same form or very similar forms. A few Russian prefixes (не-, низ-, около-, под-, против-, сверх-) have functioned as words other than prepositions and a handful have been formed by combining two prefixes to form what may often be regarded as a lexical unit (не-без-, не-до-, о-без- and possibly рас-пре-).

The etymology of native suffixes is generally very unclear. Unlike most prefixes, they have never been used as free-standing words and have rarely acquired sufficient lexical individuality to enable them to be related to elements in non-Slavonic languages. Among the more probable etymologies so far established are those connecting Russian -ск- with English *-ish*, Russian -арь with Latin *-arius*. In the majority of cases suffixes have been formed through the combination of older suffixes with determinative (lexically classifying) elements, as in *rad-os + ti (> ра́дость), and etymological links with suffixes in other languages are obscured for this reason also.

G. *The productiveness of affixes*

Productiveness is the term used to describe the frequency with which an affix is used at the present time to form new words. The adjectival suffix -ов-/-ев- (as in торго́вый) is called *very productive* because it is used to form adjectives from the stems of nouns of all kinds, because these adjectives express a wide range of meanings (relative, qualitative) and, largely as a result of these two factors, because it is found in a very large number of new adjectives. The adjectival suffix -яв-/-ав- (as in дыря́вый) is called *non-productive* because it is not used, and has not been used during this century, to form adjectives. In this work four degrees of productiveness are distinguished: very productive (VP), productive (P), weakly productive (WP), non-productive (NP). The degree of productiveness of every affix in each of its lexical functions is indicated in §9. Only affixes possessing considerable vigour (very productive or productive affixes) in at least one lexical function are dealt with in detail in §8.

Productiveness is not dependent upon any single factor. Lexically synonymous affixes with the same range of applicability may (and normally do) differ in productiveness, e.g. -их-а (as in слони́ха) is P, but -иц-а (as in льви́ца) is NP. This difference in productiveness is the result of the increased use of one affix at the expense of another, part of the elimination of duplication of functions in affixes that has been under way for the last two hundred years. Difference in the productiveness of two affixes that are not lexically synonymous is easily explained: there is not (and cannot be) a great demand for the noun suffix -ак/-як denoting persons grouped according to nationality (as in the pejorative австрия́к), but the noun and adjective prefix архи- (as in архинеле́пый, 'quite nonsensical') can be used meaningfully with any qualitative adjective and with any noun (such as жу́лик) the use of which implies an emotive assessment.

The productiveness of an affix is limited by internal or external factors, or by both. Internal factors are those independent of the environment of the affix and comprise (1) lexical specialization and (2) the etymology of the affix. These may be dealt with separately.

(1) An increase in specialization, a narrowing of lexical function, means a decrease in *applicability*, that is, a decrease in the number of situations in which an affix may be used and in the number of stems to which it may be attached. The degree of specialization in affixes varies widely. The most abstract adjectival suffixes -н-, -ов-/-ев-, -ск- may theoretically be combined with the stem of any noun in the language to express relationship, quality and (often) possession. The noun suffixes -ен-ие/-н-ие, -ость, of only slightly less general meaning, are used to form nouns of abstract meaning from most verb and adjective stems (e.g. замеча́ние, весёлость). At the other end of the scale of applicability are affixes of very precise meaning such as -ищ-е (indicating the site of an action or object, as in пожа́рище, городи́ще) or -н-ин (adjective suffix denoting family relationship, as in му́жнин брат).

(2) The etymology of an affix is important in the determination of its productiveness. There is a persistent tendency in Russian to associate 'foreign' (i.e. recently borrowed) affixes with 'foreign' stems with the result that for the most part affixes taken from western European languages are rarely used with 'native' stems. Indeed, some imported affixes are not even recognized as such and are not used with native stems (e.g. аб-, ад-; -ан (-ец, -ск-), -ив (-н-), -уаль (-н-) as in абъюра́ция, адду́ктор; америка́нец,

америка́нский, прогресси́вный, интеллектуа́льный). Of the imported affixes that have become perceived as such relatively few have become more than marginally productive in the formation of new words with 'Russian' stems. The prefixes анти-, архи-, контр(а)-, псевдо- and the suffixes -ёр, -изм, -ист, -фикация are used frequently with 'Russian' stems (as in антиобще́ственный, 'anti-social', архиопа́сный, 'very dangerous', контруда́р, 'a counter-blow', псевдонаро́дный, 'pseudo-popular, -folk', ухажёр, 'a boy friend', большеви́зм, 'bolshevism', связи́ст, 'a signaller', теплофика́ция, 'introduction of a heating system'). The remaining 'foreign' affixes are either used almost exclusively with 'foreign' stems, or so little used that one can draw no conclusions regarding their productiveness. Only in technical vocabularies (e.g. that of chemistry) are 'foreign' affixes frequently met with and even here their productiveness is suspect as they are usually imported together with a 'foreign' stem.

Productiveness is in large part determined also by external influences. The need or lack of need for any morpheme in a language is due not only to its own lexical and grammatical significance but also to the position it occupies in the patterns of the language. These patterns may be separated for examination into phonemic, lexical, grammatical and stylistic systems, but in the living language no such separation exists, each system being involved with the others. The productiveness of any affix in Russian (and in English) depends upon two sets of external relationships within the systems of the language, (1) upon correspondences with other affixes, and (2) upon associations with stems. These relationships have been created haphazardly despite a certain consistency of motivation (desire for economy and for ease of association of idea with expression) and in no case are they completely regular.

(1) Correspondences with other affixes are of two kinds. The value of an affix depends to some extent (*a*) upon its dispensability, i.e. on the existence of synonymous affixes, and (*b*) upon its use as a regular lexical or grammatical alternative to non-synonymous affixes.

(*a*) Affixes with even the broadest lexical meaning may become unproductive through permanent attachment to a small group of stems united by a common meaning, a common origin or a common phonetic peculiarity. Alternatively, any affix may decline in productiveness as the result of competition from other affixes of similar meaning. The latter process, the squeezing out of all but one of a group of affixes of synonymous meaning from combination with a given stem, has been observed on a wide front during the last two hundred years. The situation is now almost static, there being few doublets such as абрико́сный/абрико́совый (apricot). But lack of productiveness may be due not only to decline but also to non-development. Many affixes (such as the qualitatives -л-яв-, -яв-/-ав- as in вертля́вый, дыря́вый) have not been attached to any particular group of stems, yet have failed to find wide acceptance, probably because their functions are performed by other forms. In the present case the functions of -л-яв- or -яв-/-ав- are also performed by the suffix -ист-, as in волни́стый (wavy), which alone of the three is attached to new stems (it is used with the names of chemical elements as an equivalent to English *-ous*). The prefix супер- is found with only one stem of Slavonic origin (in суперобло́жка, 'a dust jacket'), probably because its functions are duplicated by сверх-, which was well established before the importation of foreign words with the former prefix.

(*b*) Nearly all stems may be used with more than one affix. Some pairs or larger groups of affixes are met with again and again in combination with the same stems and it can be seen that these have formed almost regular correspondences. In some cases these correspondences are created or strengthened by the formation of one affixed form from another, with or without previous deaffixation (e.g. -ин-ец/-ин-ск- as in я́лтинец, 'a man from Yalta', from я́лтинский). In other cases it is not possible to say that one word is derived from another by any one of a group of affixes as two or more words appear to have come into existence at once. This phenomenon is especially common among imported affixes which may be borrowed in groups rather than singly, e.g. -ировать and -ант/-ент as in оккупи́ровать, оккупа́нт, ассисти́ровать, ассисте́нт; -(а/и)ц-ия and -(а/и)т-ор as in опера́ция, опера́тор, колониза́ция, колониза́тор; -изм and -ист as in тури́зм, тури́ст, социали́зм, социали́ст.

In correspondences of this kind suffixes are usually distinguished by grammatical function (e.g. -ин-ец/-ин-ск- express a noun/adjective opposition), although lexical differences are also present. The few pairs of prefixes found in correspondence are opposed by reason of their lexical content only, e.g. суб- and супер-, в-/во- and вы-, макро- and микро-.

The productiveness of all synonymous affixes is reduced to some extent. In the case of affixes in correspondence with others of differing functions productiveness may be said to be increased, as any new formation with one affix of a pair or group makes likely the creation of forms with the other affixes.

(2) There is a tendency in all affixes to become associated with one group of stems in particular. The group may be large (cf. the association of -тель-н- with stems of transitive verbs or the association of -ист- with the stems of nouns denoting concrete objects) or small (cf. the association of -ч-еств-о with the stems of adjectives in -ч-еск- or the association of -ат- (-ат[1]-, I, see §9) with noun stems in -к, -ц only). The size of the group, and thus of the range of combinations into which an affix can enter, is determined by the lexical (and, to a certain extent, grammatical) properties of the stems or by their phonetic structure. These features may be illustrated separately although the lexical and grammatical contents of a stem are always interacting.

(*a*) Stems may be predisposed to combination with certain affixes because of their lexical meaning. The stems of verbs denoting action of which the speaker disapproves (e.g. вози́ться, ма́зать, руга́ть) combine with the affix -н-я (возня́, мазня́, ругня́) to make abstract nouns. The stems of nouns denoting animals are used with the suffix -ён-ыш to form the names of the young of these animals (утёныш, гусёныш, зверёныш). The stems of adjectives and verbs denoting prolonged actions or characteristic features (e.g. ре́зв-ый, ста́р-ый, гор-ева́ть/-юет) are used with the suffix -ух-а/-юх-а (I, see §9) to form the names of persons (резву́ха, стару́ха, горю́ха). The frequency of the affixes -н-я, -ён-ыш and -ух-а/юх-а (I, see §9) is therefore limited by the number of words in use in the above lexical categories, and the productiveness of these affixes depends largely (there are further limiting factors) on the number of words left in each category that have not so far combined with them.

(*b*) The grammatical function of the word from which a stem is taken may prevent the combination of that stem with a given affix. Most affixes are attached to stems of words belonging to only one grammatical category (e.g. nouns, verbs, adjectives) and occasionally there is some degree of specialization. The noun suffix -т-ие (-т-ье)/-т-ьё can be attached only to the infinitive stem of transitive verbs, as in разви́тие, бритьё. On the other hand, the adjective suffix -ч- is attached only to the present stem of intransitive verbs, as in лежа́чий, вися́чий, колю́чий. It is unlikely, however, that the grammatical function of the words providing the stems can seriously affect the productiveness of any affix. No matter how strong or weak the grammatical function of an affix, it is capable of operating in combination with words of very broad classes. Affixes which create nouns from the stems of verbs (such as -ец, -тель, -щик/-чик as in купе́ц, граби́тель, продавщи́к) operate over the full range of transitive verbs (this is the only purely grammatical condition imposed on verb stems before they can become eligible for use with affixes). Affixes which create nouns from the stems of adjectives (such as -к-а as in овся́нка, 'porridge') or which create adjectives from the stems of nouns or verbs (such as -аст-/-яст- as in глаза́стый, -лив- as in пугли́вый) are not affected in their power of combination with stems by any grammatical property of the words from which the stems are taken.

(*c*) Certain affixes produce phonetic changes (hardening, softening, mutation) in the stems to which they are attached (see §4E). Other affixes behave more passively, adapting themselves to the phonetic conditions at the beginning or end of stems. This adaptation, which may be described alternatively as the product of an influence exerted by the stem, takes one of three forms: (1) *vowel-change* (e.g. -ов- > -ев- as in ноздрева́тый, 'porous', cf. углова́тый, 'angular'), (2) *assimilation* (e.g. без- > бес- as in бесконе́чный, 'infinite', cf. безвре́дный, 'harmless') or (3) *insertion of a vowel* (e.g. в- > во- as in воплоще́ние, 'an embodiment', cf. вклад, 'a contribution'). Insertion of a consonant is uncommon and may probably be explained morphologically (as in the case of -ль- in бели́льщик, 'a bleacher'). In one instance (the де-/дез- alternation) the insertion of the consonant antedates the borrowing of the morpheme into Russian, as in дезинтегра́ция. Limitation of productiveness occurs when adaptation does not take place and affixes are replaced in certain phonetic contexts by synonyms. The suffix -щик cannot be used (with very rare exceptions) after the consonants т/д, с/з, and is replaced in these positions by -чик, as in счётчик (a meter), разно́счик (a hawker). Affixes suffering limitations of this sort are few in number and although the limitations may in some cases be severe (as in the case of -ен-к-а, which is added only to stems ending in -с, -з or -х), the phonetic structure of stems must be considered no more than an occasional, and so minor, factor in limiting productiveness over the whole range of affixes.

H. *The analysis and translation of affixed words*

Nouns and adjectives in Russian may be simple (год; бе́лый), simple and affixed (моло́чник, прие́зд, похо́дка; маслянистый, архиглу́пый, подзе́мный), compound (металлоло́м; чернобро́вый) or compound and affixed (пчелово́дство, управдо́м, неплодоро́дность; низкосо́ртный, неплодоро́дный). Rapid and successful translation of a strange word depends both on identification of the elements of the word as root(s)/stem(s), affixes, link-vowels and terminations and on understanding of the meaning of each of the elements so identified.

The analysis of affixed words, whether simple or compound, is best undertaken by isolating (*a*) terminations, (*b*) affixes, (*c*) stem or stems, in that order. Link-vowels (the meaningless vowels о and е sometimes found between stems) may be ignored for present purposes. Terminations will certainly be recognized and (except in a few instances, such as in бра́тнин, 'brother's', пере́дняя, 'hall') will serve to distinguish nouns from adjectives. The initial syllable of the word and the syllable preceding the termination (or the final syllable, where there is no termination) should be sought in a complete list of affixes (e.g. §9 of the present work): absence from this list indicates that the syllable in question is a stem or part of a stem. The separation of terminations and initial and final affixes leaves a form which must consist of either (*a*) a stem or (*b*) two or more stems, any two of which may be joined by a link-vowel or separated by a prefix or suffix (as in низ-к-о-со́рт-н-ый, радио-при-ём-ник, 'a radio receiver').

Recognition (isolation) of meaningful suffixes may present some difficulty to the student who has had little practice in the analysis of forms. In the case of a word of which no part is known (say, точи́льня) it is probably best to seek in the list groups of letters taken from the end of the word, beginning with a group of three letters (here -ьня) as this is, orthographically, the average length of a suffix. Groups of four, two and one letter should then be sought (here -льня, -ня, -я) and the longest form given in the list should be taken as the suffix. Because of the possibility of alternative analyses (as in революци-он-éр and революц-ион-éр, вишнёв-к-а and вишн-ёв-к-а, груз-ови́к and грузов-и́к) it is important to confirm the correctness of one's choice by making sure that the stem preceding the suffix(es) is intact. In the present case the stem точи-, left after the removal of -ль-н-я, is clearly that of the verb точи́ть (to grind, sharpen).

Nearly all suffixes more than four letters in length are, or were originally, multiple suffixes (usually adjective suffix plus noun suffix, or noun suffix plus adjective suffix). In eight cases out of ten only two suffixes are used together, even a long form like -ничество being reducible to two lexical elements, -ник- and -ств-о. The final (pre-termination) element of a multiple suffix may only be one of a fairly restricted list, this making for the easy recognition of such multiple forms. The list follows.

Noun suffixes

-ер, -ец, -изм, -ик, -ика, -ин[1], -ин[3], -ист[1], -ист[2], -их-а, -иц-а, -ич, -ищ-е, -ия, -к-а, -н-а, -ник, -ниц-а, -н-я, -ок, -ор, -ость, -ств-о, -ш-а, -щик, -щин-а, -щиц-а, -ыш, -ье, -ьё.

Adjective suffixes

-енн-, -ит[4]-, -к-, -н[1]-, -нн-, -ов[2]-, -ск-, -ь-, -яв-.

The second element of a multiple suffix modifies the meaning expressed by the combination of the stem and first element (which frequently exist together as a word, as do the stem and first element of води́-тель-ств-о, 'leadership', and води́-тель-ск-ий, 'leader's'), functioning in precisely the same way as it does when a single suffix. The suffixes -ств-о and -ск- have the same functions in произво́дство (production) and городско́й (urban) as in the examples given above. Translation is effected by deciding which of the possible meanings of each affix contained in a word is most appropriate (or probable) considering the meaning of the stem to which it is joined. The range of meanings (both lexical and grammatical) of any affix is limited and the meanings of the more common affixes will soon become familiar through repeated reference to the list. Memorizing the functions of the very productive and productive affixes (see §8), which happen to be those occurring most often, will repay the effort required.

While it is of practical value to memorize the functions of all affixes used in Russian nouns and adjectives, it is useless to attempt to learn the meanings of all the stems that may be met with as there are at least six thousand different roots upon which these stems are based. Considerable progress can be achieved, however, by limiting active vocabulary learning to the acquisition of words occurring frequently and by cultivating the habit of analysing new words met with in reading and of relating them where possible to the basic vocabulary.[1]

5

DERIVATORY PROCEDURES: III

A. *Compounding* (*composition*). *General*

Compound words are words containing two or more stems. In addition to the stems, a compound word may contain affixes, and the stems may be joined together by a link-vowel or link-vowels. The first component normally bears a secondary stress, the main stress falling on the final stem.

The stems in a compound word in Russian may appear in full, as in работ-о-спосóб-н-ость (efficiency), or мягк-о-сердéч-н-ый (kindly, soft-hearted). Frequently, however, abbreviations are used in place of complete stems. These abbreviations may consist of no more than the initial letters of stems, which may be pronounced separately, as in Лф (элэ́ф = Ленингрáдский филиáл), or together, as in ТАСС (= Телегрáфное агéнтство Совéтского Союза). More commonly used, although less numerous, are less drastic abbreviations. These may be regarded as abbreviations of whole words; e.g. -мех- at the beginning or in the middle of a word stands for механизи́рованный or механи́ческий, as in мехчáсти, дормехбáза (= дорóжная механи́ческая бáза). The formal identity of some of these abbreviations with affixes can lead the foreign student into difficulties: пред-, for instance, can stand for председáтель, and под- may imply подвóдный (cf. предколхóза, подлóдка). As can be seen from the above examples, any number of components in a Russian compound may be

[1] A basic vocabulary may be collected from a dictionary in which words are listed in order of frequency of occurrence. The most recent such dictionary is Shteinfeldt (1963).

abbreviated and great complexity is reached when these components are arranged in an order not corresponding to the sentence order of the words when used in full. Главсельстройпрое́кт stands for Гла́вное управле́ние по проекти́рованию се́льских зда́ний и сооруже́ний при Госуда́рственном комите́те по дела́м строи́тельства СССР. An accurate analysis of such a giant is impossible, as many parts of the phrase which it represents are missing, although it is not difficult to get a rough idea of the meaning of the word once the components are separated and understood. Each of the units глав, сель, строй, проект represents an idea, as do the words гла́вный, се́льский, строи́тельство, проекти́рование of which they are abbreviations. The order of importance of these ideas and the equivalence or subordination of any one to another are not, however, indicated by the order in which they are expressed, and the meaning of the word as a whole must be learnt before it can be used. Abbreviated compounds are usually *ad hoc* creations, each being known in isolation by its users, and there is no guarantee that any new compound of this type, e.g. *Главгорстройпроект, will be understood at once by a native speaker. Several dictionaries of abbreviations exist to give explanations which are unnecessary in the case of non-abbreviated compounds: the largest of these are listed in the bibliography (Koritsky, 1963; Scheitz, 1961).

For the foreign learner separated from his dictionary two facts may be of comfort. First, a limited number of abbreviations occur very frequently in Russian compound words: these are listed under §5D and will repay memorizing. Secondly, most abbreviations, including all the common ones mentioned above, tend to occur in the same positions in all compounds. глав- (= гла́вный or гла́вное управле́ние) is nearly always initial, -пред (= представи́тель as distinct from пред- as in предрассу́док, 'a prejudice') is always final. Abbreviated adjectives normally stand before abbreviated nouns, as in Детги́з (= де́тский + госуда́рственное изда́тельство), физо́рг (= физкульту́рный организа́тор) and -сельстрой- in the example given above. This permits a considerable degree of understanding in nearly all cases through the construction of 'unreal' expansions of the abbreviated compounds. *Детское государственное издательство does not exist in Russian but it is helpful to construct it as an aid to understanding.

B. *The analysis and translation of compound words*

As the preceding description of compounds in Russian indicates, the study of these words is more complicated and usually less rewarding for the foreign student than that of simple (non-compound) words with affixes.

The meaning of a compound word cannot be obtained by adding together the meanings of its components, which is to a large extent the procedure to be followed in analysing affixed words. The relationship between the two or more parts of a compound word is largely expressed by the linear positions of these parts, and it is the difficulty of remembering the significance of the various possible positions that creates the largest problem in the study of compounds. Position is significant in the attachment of affixes to stems in that there are general features in the relationship of prefixes to stems that distinguish them clearly from suffixes (and infixes). Nevertheless, as every affix is found exclusively in one position relative to the stems (e.g. за is always a prefix, иц-а is always a suffix), the position of affixes may be learned together with their forms. This does not apply in the case of the components of compound words. The use of affixes in compound words adds a complication, as these may refer either to the whole of the compound (as does -н- in низкосóртный, 'of poor quality') or to only one of the components (as does -н- in судостроúтельный, 'shipbuilding'; -ис- (-из-) in времяисчислéние, 'a calendar, chronology').

Students meeting a new compound word in Russian are faced with three problems:

(1) The correct division of the word into its components (see pp. 42–3).

(2) The understanding of the meaning of each of these components (see pp. 44–7).

(3) The understanding of the relationships between the components (see pp. 47, 52–66).

Unless all of these difficulties are solved no compound word in Russian can be translated with any confidence. Owing to the limitless number of possible components an exhaustive treatment of these is impossible, but enough can be said under each of the above headings to make serious mistakes unlikely. An understanding of the relationships of components to one another is especially important.

(1) The structure of compounds in Russian varies considerably. All compound words must contain at least two stems or parts of stems. This means that every compound word contains two elements which are nominal, adjectival, adverbial or verbal in origin. In addition to these elements a compound may contain affixes and link-vowels. Affixes are meaningful (they have a lexical and/or grammatical function). Link-vowels are not, and are possibly inserted in order to facilitate pronunciation. If we represent the stems (or abbreviated stems) of a compound word by numerals, affixes by *p* (prefix) and *s* (suffix), and link-vowels by *o*, the following formulae represent the most usual combinations incorporating two stems only. Symbols for affixes are separated by hyphens from those for stems (or abbreviated stems) only in cases where the affixes are not 'etymologically' attached to the stems.

1-2	НД (эндэ́) (= наро́дная дружи́на) (a volunteer police organization)
	совхо́з (= сове́тское хозя́йство) (a state farm)
	спорттова́ры (sports equipment)
p1-2	управдо́м (= управля́ющий до́мом) (a house-manager)
1-2-s	двуство́лка (a double-barrelled gun)
1-0-2	коротковоло́сый (short-haired)
	пылесо́с (a vacuum-cleaner)
	языкове́д (a philologist)
1-0-p2	металлозаво́д (a metallurgical plant)
1-0-2-s	длинново́лновый (long-wave)

A number of poorly represented combinations (e.g. *p-1-2-s*, *p1-2-s*, *p-1-0-2*) are omitted from the list.

The size of this series of possibilities shows that little is to be gained by relying on the probability of occurrence of any common pattern. However, certain of the elements making up each of the patterns (the prefixes, link-vowels and suffixes) recur frequently and may be readily recognized. With a very few exceptions (some foreign prefixes and a handful of NP suffixes, e.g. вице-, экс-; -б-а, -с-а), all affixes may be used in composition. As there are no affixes peculiar to compound words the prefixes and suffixes in such words may be readily isolated, together with the stems to which they are attached. There are only two link-vowels, о (which follows a hard consonant) and е (after a soft consonant). Recognition of affixes and link-vowels makes the analysis of most two-stem compounds a simple matter.

A severe and often insuperable difficulty is presented by the abbreviation of stems. The difficulty arises in all cases of compounds with more than two stems (e.g. *1s-2s-3s* минвнешто́рг, *1s-2s-3s* РО́СТА, *1-p2s-3s-4* СССР, *p1s-p2ss-3-4s-p5* НИИТеплоприбо́р etc.).[1] The rarity of link-vowels and suffixes due to this practice of drastic abbreviation makes the analysis of many of the longer compounds very difficult (and often impossible). Ease of analysis (and of understanding) depends upon the degree of contraction practised. Where stems (and stems-plus-affixes) are reduced to initials (e.g. СССР, ЛОНТО́, НТОНГП; НТОЛеспро́м[2]) no analysis is possible and the word conveys nothing unless it has previously been learnt. A single initial can represent a stem (as in *С*ССР), a suffixed stem (as in СС*С*Р), a prefixed-and-suffixed stem (as in НТОНГ*П*) or (less commonly) a prefixed stem, as in *З*ИЛ (Заво́д и́мени Ле́нина). Not infrequently a single letter stands for more than one word, as in Л*О*НТО́, where *О* must indicate областно́е правле́ние. Sometimes a set of initials is used as an abbreviation for a phrase in which one or more non-nominal and non-verbal word is omitted, as in МПВП (эмпэвэпэ́), Междунаро́дная передвижна́я вы́ставка прибо́ров и средств измере́ния (International Travelling Exhibition of Measuring Devices).

The situation is a little more hopeful where less radical contractions are concerned (e.g. Главсельстройпрое́кт), although the irregular representation of affixes and the non-representation of auxiliary words and conjunctions persists. We are helped in the analysis of compounds containing contractions which are not merely initials by the frequent use of set forms to represent longer words of various grammatical categories. Глав- may stand for гла́вный or for the two words гла́вное правле́ние. Сель- may stand for се́льский, or се́льское хозя́йство, or сельскохозя́йственный. Строй- may stand for строи́тельный or строи́тельство.

[1] минвнешто́рг = Министе́рство вне́шней торго́вли, Ministry of Foreign Trade.
РО́СТА = Росси́йкое телегра́фное аге́нтство, Russian Telegraph Agency.
НИИТеплоприбо́р = Нау́чно-иссле́довательский институ́т теплоэнерге́тического приборострое́ния, Scientific Research Institute of Instrument-making for Heat-power Engineering.

[2] ЛОНТО́ = Ленингра́дское областно́е правле́ние Нау́чно-техни́ческого о́бщества, The Leningrad Province Board of the Scientific and Technical Society.
НТОНГП = Нау́чно-техни́ческое о́бщество нефтяно́й и га́зовой промы́шленности, The Scientific and Technical Society for the Oil and Gas Industry.
НТОЛеспро́м = Нау́чно-техни́ческое о́бщество лесно́й промы́шленности, The Scientific and Technical Society for the Timber Industry.

(2) A number of forms, which may be considered as stems and which are not contracted, are omitted from most dictionaries, as they do not exist as words in their own right. These *units of composition* or *bound morphemes* are distinct from affixes in that they possess nominal or adjectival meaning, but may be compared with affixes from a structural point of view in that they normally precede or follow other stems (nouns such as перевáл, 'a mountain-pass', разрéз, 'a section', being considered as derived from prefixed verbs). Exceptions to the rule requiring the presence of another stem before or after a unit of composition are a dozen or so nouns in само- (e.g. самовáр, 'samovar', самогóн, 'hooch', самокáт, 'a pushbike') and a few anomalous forms such as вездехóд (a jeep). Unlike affixes, however, they are normally separated from these other stems by a link-vowel. Like words and abbreviations, units of composition may be affixed (e.g. мясо-рýб-к-а, 'a mincing-machine', счетовóд-ств-о, 'accountancy'), the suffixes -ия, -к-а, -н-я, -ств-о and -ье/-ие, and -н- (less often -ов-, -ск-) being characteristic with these stems. Examples of units of composition follow. It will be noticed that it is possible in the case of native roots to regard the units of composition as deaffixed but that these units are distinct from contractions in that they have a meaning of their own and do not represent longer words. They are capable of entering into compounds expressing entirely new ideas (e.g. моторóллер, 'a motor-scooter', which cannot be considered as a contraction of motóрный рóллер as this combination is never used). Units which form homophones with words or contractions of similar meaning are marked (H).

(*a*) *Deverbal units* (*of nominal meaning*)

-вод: экскурсовóд (a guide), cf. экскýрсия (a trip), водúть (to lead).
-мер: землемéр (a surveyor), cf. землЯ́ (earth, land), мéрить (to measure).
-род (H): углерóд (carbon), cf. ýголь (coal), родúть (to bear).

(*b*) *Borrowed, originally deverbal, units* (*of nominal meaning*)

-граф: библиóграф (a bibliographer).
-скоп: телескóп (a telescope).
-фил: славянофúл (a Slavophile), cf. славЯ́не (the Slavs).

(*c*) *Borrowed, originally denominal and deadjectival units* (*of adjectival meaning*)

гидро-: гидросамолёт (a seaplane), cf. самолёт (an aeroplane).
мото-: мотодрезúна (a motorized trolley), cf. дрезúна (a trolley).
фото-: фотокóпия (a photo-copy), cf. кóпия (a copy).

Most of these units are of foreign origin and have in many cases been borrowed together with the stem to which they are attached (as is the case with германофо́б, термо́метр; аэродина́мика, фотохи́мия, etc.). No units of native origin (produced in Russian by deaffixation) are used initially or are derived from nouns or adjectives. No difficulty is found in understanding the borrowed units of composition as they are all property common to English and Russian (allowing for minor phonetic modifications). The units of native origin may not be recognized. The most common of these are listed first.

C. *List of the most common units of composition (bound morphemes)*

Units which form homophones with free-standing words or contractions of similar meaning are marked (H).

(*a*) *Deverbal units* (*of nominal meaning*)

-БОЙ (H) as in			
китобо́й	скотобо́й-н-я	compare	бить
a whaler, whale hunter	an abattoir		to strike, kill
-ВАР (H) as in			
сталева́р			вари́ть
a steel founder			to boil, found
-ВЕД as in			
почвове́д	языкове́д-ен-ие		ведь
a soil scientist	philology		you know, you see
-ВОД as in			
экскурсово́д			води́ть
a guide, courier			to lead
скотово́д	пчелово́д-ств-о		раз-води́ть
a cattle breeder	beekeeping		to breed
-ВОЗ (H) as in			
лесово́з			вози́ть
a log transporter			to transport
электрово́з			
an electric locomotive			
-ДЕЛ as in			
виноде́л	маслоде́л-ие		де́лать
a winemaker	the butter industry		to make
-КОЛ (H) as in			
ледоко́л			коло́ть
an icebreaker			to stab, split
-КОП as in			
землеко́п			копа́ть
a navvy			to dig

-КОС as in		
сенокóс		compare косúть
haymaking		to mow
-ЛОВ (Н) as in		
тигролóв	зверолóв-ств-о	ловúть
a tiger hunter	trapping	to catch
-МЕР as in		
землемéр		мéрить
a surveyor		to measure
-МЁТ as in		
пулемёт		метáть
a machine-gun		to throw
-ПАД as in		
водопáд		пáдать
a waterfall		to fall
-ПИСЬ[1] as in		
машúнопись (f.)		писáть
typewriting		to write
-ПРО-ВОД (Н) as in		
нефтепровóд		про-водúть
an oil pipe-line		to lead through
-РЕЗ (Н) as in		
винторéз		рéзать
a screw-cutting machine		to cut
-РОД (Н) as in		
водорóд		родúть
hydrogen		to breed, bear
-РУБ as in		
ледорýб		рубúть
an ice-axe		to chop
-СОС as in		
пылесóс		сосáть
a vacuum-cleaner		to suck
-ХОД (Н) as in		
теплохóд		ходúть
a motor-ship		to walk

-БОЙ is unexpected. One would expect -БЕЙ here, and the present form may be due to analogy with forms such as закрóй (from закры́ть) or may be taken from an unrecorded form of the verb.

[1] This form is exceptional in that it is used in the formation of feminine nouns ending in a soft consonant and in which stress is non-final.

(*b*) *Borrowed units* (*of nominal meaning*)

-ГРАФ as in геóграф (a geographer), гидрогрáф-ия (hydrography), телегрáф (a telegraph)
-МАН англомáн (an Anglomaniac), галломáн-ия (Gallomania)
-МЕТР (Н) хронóметр (a chronometer), антропомéтр-ия (anthropometry)
-СКОП спектроскóп (a spectroscope), микроскоп-и́я (miscroscopy)
-ФИЛ русофи́л (a Russophile), англофи́ль-ств-о (Anglophilism)
-ФОБ германофóб (a Germanophobe), юдофóб-ств-о (Anti-Semitism)
-ФОН (Н) ксилофóн (a xylophone), стереофон-и́я (stereophony)

(*c*) *Borrowed denominal and deadjectival units* (*of adjectival meaning*)

АГРО- (Н) агрогóрод (an agricultural centre)
АЭРО- аэропóрт (an airport)
ГИДРО- (Н) гидроплáн (a hydroplane, hydrofoil)
КИНО- (Н) киноарти́ст (a screen actor)
МОТО- (Н) мотодрези́на (a motorized trolley)
ФОТО- (Н) фотокóпия (a photocopy)

Contractions, unlike the units of composition, are catered for by specialized dictionaries. The titles of the most modern and complete of these are given in the bibliography. The list of abbreviated stems which follows in §5D includes only those likely to be met with in reading non-technical texts. No list of initials is provided as a single letter may have very many meanings. The student is referred to the dictionaries mentioned in the bibliography.

(3) Once the meaning of each component of a compound is known there is no guarantee that the whole word will become intelligible. Immediate understanding follows naturally when uncontracted components are in a linear relationship identical with that presented by the words when written separately and with the appropriate affixes and endings. Черноволóсый, analysed as черн + о + волос + ый, may be compared with чёрные вóлосы and translated at once as 'black-haired'. Difficulties arise from two sources: (*a*) from complexity in the relationship between the components (whether whole or abbreviated stems) of compounds, and (*b*) from the non-representation in the compound of ideas essential to its understanding. This last applies only to compounds made up of abbreviated stems. These problems are discussed in detail in §5E.

D. *List of the most common abbreviations used in compound words*

Hyphens before and after abbreviations indicate whether the given forms may be used initially, finally, or in any position. Thus авиа- is found only in an initial position and -арм appears only at the end of words, but -авто- may be used initially, medially or finally.

авиа-	авиацио́нный	авиапо́чта	air-mail
авто-	автомати́ческий	авторучка	a fountain-pen
-авто-	автомоби́льный	автозаво́д	a car factory
агро-	агрономи́ческий	агрохи́мия	agrochemistry
адм-	администрати́вный	адмотде́л	an administrative section
академ-	академи́ческий	Академкни́га	the Academy of Sciences publishing house
-арм	а́рмия	команда́рм	an army commander
астро-	астрономи́ческий	астрофи́зика	astrophysics
био-	биологи́ческий	биото́пливо	a bio-fuel
бое-	боево́й	боеподгото́вка	military training
борт-	бортово́й	бортпроводни́ца	a stewardess
броне-	брони́ро́ванный	бронепо́езд	an armoured train
-быт-	бытово́й	Мосгорбытсна́б	Bureau for the Supply of Domestic Appliances, Moscow
вело-	велосипе́дный	велоспо́рт	cycling
-внеш-	вне́шний	внешторгба́нк	Bank for Foreign Trade
-вод-	во́дный	Главводпу́ть	Central Waterways Board
	во́дный тра́нспорт	Главво́д	Central Water Transport Board
воен-	вое́нный	военинжене́р	a military engineer
ген-	генера́льный	гензове́т	General Council
гео-	геологи́ческий	георазве́дка	a geological survey
гидро-	гидравли́ческий	гидронасо́с	a hydraulic pump
	гидротехни́ческий	гидросооруже́ние	hydraulic engineering
	гидроэлектри́ческий	гидроста́нция	a hydroelectric power station

глав-	гла́вный	главвра́ч	a head physician
-глав-	гла́вное управле́ние	Главга́з	Central Gas Board
-гор-	городско́й	Мосгорсове́т	Moscow City Council
-гос-	госуда́рственный	госбезопа́сность	State Security
дет-	де́тский	детса́д	a kindergarten
дом-	дома́шний	домрабо́тница	a maid, domestic help
	домо́вый	домко́м	a house-committee
-драм-	драмати́ческий	облдрамтеа́тр	a provincial theatre
жен-	же́нский	женотде́л	Women's Department
-жил-	жили́щный	райжилуправле́ние	Local Housing Authority
	жило́й	жилпло́щадь	living space
зав-	заве́дующий	завка́федрой	a head of a university department
-зав-	заводско́й	завко́м	a factory committee
-здрав-	здравоохране́ние	здравпу́нкт	Health Centre
-зем-	земе́льный	земфо́нд	Land Reserve
-издат	изда́тельство	Воениздáт	Military Publishing House
-ин-	иностра́нный	Мининде́л	Ministry for Foreign Affairs
-интерн	интернациона́л	Спортинте́рн	an international sports organization
ист-	истори́ческий	истфа́к	Historical Faculty
ком-	команди́р	комди́в	a divisional commander
	кома́ндный	комсоста́в	a military Staff
	коммунисти́ческий	компа́ртия	Communist Party
-ком	комисса́р	военко́м	a military commissar
	коми́ссия	чрезко́м	an extraordinary commission
	комите́т	местко́м	a local Party committee
край-	краево́й	крайздра́в	Regional Health Authority
культ-	культу́рный		
	культу́рно-просвети́тельный	культпохо́д	an educational trip, excursion
Лен-	Ленингра́дский	Ленгорсове́т	Leningrad City Council

-лес-,			
лесо-	лесно́й	лесхо́з	forestry
	лесозаготови́тельный	лесозаво́д	a sawmill
лит-	литерату́рный	литфа́к	Faculty of Literature, Letters
-лит-	литерату́ра	Гослитизда́т	State Publishing House
-маг	магази́н	универма́г	a department store
металло-	металли́ческий	металлоизде́лия	metal goods
-мех-	механизи́рованный	мотомехвойска́	motorized and mechanized troops
	механи́ческий	мехба́за	a servicing base
-мин-	министе́рство	минздра́в	Ministry of Health
Мос-	Моско́вский	Моска́бель	Moscow Cable Works
мото-	моторизо́ванный	мотодиви́зия	a motorized division
	мото́рный	мотоло́дка	a motorboat
-нар-	наро́дный	совнархо́з	Economic Council
нац-	национа́льный	нацменьшинство́	a national minority
обл-	областно́й	облсове́т	a provincial council
орг-	организацио́нный	оргбюро́	Organization Bureau
-орг	организа́тор	парто́рг	a party organizer
-парт-	парти́йный	партбиле́т	a party card
пед-	педагоги́ческий	пединститу́т	a teachers' training college
полит-	полити́ческий	политрабо́та	political work
-пом-	помо́щник	помза́в	an assistant manager
пред-	председа́тель	предколхо́за	a collective farm president
-пред	представи́тель	торгпре́д	a trade representative
прод-	продово́льственный	продма́г	a grocery store
-пром-	промысло́вый	промкомбина́т	an industrial combine
	промы́шленный	промтова́ры	industrial goods
проф-	профсою́зный	профдвиже́ние	the Trade Union movement
-проф-	профессиона́льный	профсою́з	a Trade Union
-раб-	рабо́чий	рабси́ла	manpower

рай-	райо́нный	райпла́н	a local (economic) plan
-рук	руководи́тель	военру́к	a military instructor
-сан-	санита́рный	санинспе́ктор	a sanitary inspector
-сель-	се́льский	сельсове́т	a village council
-снаб-	снабже́ние	снабсбы́т	Supply and Marketing Department
сов-	сове́тский	Совинформбюро́	Soviet Information Bureau
-сов-	сове́т	совми́н	Council of Ministers
-строй-	строи́тельный	стройплоща́дка	a construction site
-строй	строи́тельство	Волгостро́й	Volga Construction Project
-тех-	техни́ческий	технадзо́р	technical supervision
-торг-	торго́вля	внешто́рг	foreign trade
	торго́вый	торготде́л	Department of Commerce
-труд-	трудово́й	трудкни́жка	a worker's record book
тур-	туристи́ческий	турба́за	a hostel for tourists
управ-	управля́ющий	управдела́ми	a director
фаб-	фабри́чный	фабко́м	a factory committee
-фак	факульте́т	медфа́к	Faculty of Medicine
физ-	физкульту́рный	физо́рг	a P.T. instructor
-физ-	физи́ческий	физхи́мия	physical chemistry
-хим-	хими́ческий	химчи́стка	dry-cleaning
-хоз-	хозя́йственный	хозрасчёт	auditing
-хоз	хозя́йство	совнархо́з	Economic Council
эконом-	экономи́ческий	экономгеогра́фия	economic geography

E. *The structure of compound words*

Despite the variety and complexity of relationships between the component stems of a compound and between these and the affixes attached to them, it is often possible to understand the relationships within a new word and so to translate it accurately. This can be done because of the regularity with which certain correspondences between (*a*) the structure of the whole, (*b*) the etymology of each component, (*c*) the function of each component, and (*d*) the meaning of the whole are found in compound words in Russian. For instance, in any compound word of structure *1-o-2-s* such as плодоро́дный or коротково́лновый two sets of relationships between the elements of the word are common. Where stem *1* is of nominal origin (as in плодоро́дный) it is normally subordinate to stem *2*, the meaning of the first delimiting that of the second as though it were the object of an action the performance or result of which is denoted by the second stem. The use of stem *1* determines more precisely the meaning of stem *2*, but the combination of these components is given grammatical direction by the affix: -н- cannot be said to refer in particular to the stem (stem *2*, -род-) to which it is attached. These relationships may be presented symbolically by a rearrangement of the structural formula: *s*(*1*//*2*). (An explanation of the auxiliary symbols /, //, (), etc., follows on pp. 55–6.) Where stem *1* is of adjectival origin (as in коротково́лновый) it is again normally subordinate to stem *2*, but the delimitation of meaning is adjectival and far more readily understood in terms of the conventional grammatical categories than is the relationship between the two stems of плодоро́дный. As in the case of плодоро́дный, the suffix refers to both components at once (contrast compounds in which stem *1* functions as an adverb, e.g. ржавокори́чневый 'rusty-brown'). The relationships between the elements of коротково́лновый may be represented by the formula *s*(*1*/*2*).

It is possible to list examples of all the types of compound which the student is likely to meet and to group these examples according to correspondences between structure, etymology and meaning. A list of this kind follows in Table 1 (p. 59). It will be seen that while the correspondences in question cannot be regarded as 'laws', they are sufficiently regular to make a close study of them valuable as an aid to translation. In keeping with this practical aim the number of compounds with abbreviated stems given in the list has been severely limited. Examples such as Детги́з and СССР illustrate only a few of the wide variety of relationships possible in compounds of this kind, but are sufficient to show the feature common to most of them (modification plus qualification of a central meaning).

The list consists of all the compound words quoted in the present work with the exception of those given in the list of abbreviations on pp. 48–51, a further fifteen nouns chosen because of structural or etymological peculiarities: вездехо́д (a jeep), спорткружо́к (a sports club), мертворождённый (stillborn), ежесу́точный (daily), красноарме́ец (a Red Army man), однообъекти́вный (single-objective), жаропро́чный (heatproof), животво́рный (life-giving), кни́жка-па́мятка (a memo-book), and six words made up of drastically abbreviated stems.

Each of the words in the list is described in four ways in order to indicate the relationships between stems, affixes and whole compounds. The descriptions concern the etymology of the stems **A**, the functions of the stems in the compound **B**, the structure of the word **C**, and the relationships between the formal elements in this structure **D**. These descriptions are written in symbols in order to save space. The following notes will make it easier to understand each description.

A and **B** are concerned with the stems of the compound and with such affixes as are attached to the stems when these are found as free-standing words. Affixes which are not of this type (that is, which belong to the compound word as a whole) and which may be termed *all-modifying* affixes are ignored in the first of these descriptions. **A** gives the etymology of each stem (with its affixes). This means the indication of the grammatical category of the word from which the stem (with affixes) is presumed to be taken. The first stem of совхо́з, сов-, is described as adjectival because it is a contraction of сове́тское. The final stem of металлозаво́д is considered in combination with its prefix to be not of verbal but of nominal origin because of the existence of заво́д as a free-standing word. The symbols a, adv, n, num, pt indicate adjective, adverb, noun, numeral and participle respectively. Units of composition (not found as free-standing words) are indicated by u. The etymology of совхо́з is thus denoted by a:n, that of металлозаво́д by n:n, that of фотоко́пия by u:n.

B ignores the etymologies of the stems, dealing only with the grammatical function of each stem within the compound. These functions are denoted by the terms adjectival, adverbial, nominal and numerical, the symbols a, adv, n, num being used, as in совхóз a:n, металлозавóд a:n, фотокóпия a:n. The presence of an all-modifying affix is indicated by enclosing the symbols within brackets, as in пятиднéвный (num:n). The use of the sign > between columns **A** and **B** implies the change in function in the stems brought together in compounds.

C and **D** are concerned with the structure of the compound and with the lexical and grammatical relationships between the elements (stems, affixes) of the word. The structural formula (column **C**) is the indication of either (*a*) in the case of compounds with non-abbreviated stems, the formal units making up the word, or (*b*) in the case of compounds with abbreviated stems, the formal units which these abbreviations most probably represent. Using the symbols *1*, *2*, etc. to indicate stems and *p*, *s*, *o* to indicate prefixes, suffixes and link-vowels respectively, the examples quoted above may be described as *p1s-2s* (совхóз), *1-o-p2* (металлозавóд), *1o-2s* (фотокóпия), *1-2-s* (пятиднéвный). Hyphens separate elements of disparate immediate origin, so that stems used with affixes previous to incorporation into compounds (e.g. -завод, *-p2*) are distinguished from stems in contiguity with all-modifying affixes (e.g. неплод-, *p-1-*, in неплодорóдный, *p-1-o-2-s*). Where link-vowels, normally represented as isolated by means of hyphens (as in землекóп, *1-o-2*), may be regarded in an alternative analysis as part of a stem, they are represented with the omission of a hyphen (as in фотокóпия *1o-2s*, not *1-o-2s*).

Compounds with drastically abbreviated stems present a problem. While СССР and ТАСС might be represented by *1234* (the suffixes of the abbreviated words being ignored), it is not possible to treat МПВП in the same way as all the initials are taken from prefixes. To preserve consistency it is necessary to use *1-p2s-3s-4* as the formula for СССР, *1s-2s-p3s-4* for ТАСС, and *pp1s-p2s-p3s-p4* for МПВП. A complication is presented by compounds such as главсельстройпроéкт in which the relationship between form and meaning is not clear. Here each of the four stems may stand for more than one form of the same word. Clearly no one formula is sure to be accurate in such cases and the resultant uncertainty is indicated by the use of question marks. (The structural formula for the above example is *1s?-2s?-3s?-4s?.*) The non-representation of words in a compound with abbreviated stems cannot be taken into consideration in writing a formula for the compound.

The formulae resulting from the application of the principles outlined above are often very unwieldy and may obscure structural similarities in compounds. To facilitate comparison, therefore, the compounds in the list are grouped according to the essential features of their structure only. By regarding affixes which are etymologically attached to stems as non-significant in our classification and by ignoring link-vowels which disappear in an alternative analysis we are able to bring together for comparison such items as: аэропо́рт (precise structural formula: *10-2*), аэродина́мика (*10-2s*), колхо́з (*1s-2s*), НД (*p1s-2s*), спорттова́ры (*1s-2*), describing them as belonging to 'structural type **1-2**'.

This arrangement of items according to structural types throws into relief the varieties of grammatical and lexical relationship existing between the components of compounds. The structural formulae quoted above are inadequate to denote relationships of these kinds as they refer only to orthographical arrangement of components. The symbols *10-2s* tell us a good deal about the functions and linear order of each of the elements of аэродина́мика but reveal little concerning the relationships between these elements.

In description **D** this gap is filled by a rewriting of the (linear) structural formula. The rewriting entails a rearrangement of the symbols *1*, *2*, etc., *p* and *s* and the omission of the symbol *o* (representing a lexically functionless element), the introduction of signs (+, /, //) to denote varieties of lexico-grammatical relationship and the use of brackets to indicate the syntactic equality of elements. The sign + denotes co-ordination as seen in the compound СССР where the words represented by the second and third initials form a co-ordinate group. Oblique strokes are used to denote subordination (non-co-ordination). An *attributive* (appositional, modifying) relationship, as in спорткружо́к where the first stem (in full, спорти́вный) expresses an attribute of the second, is denoted by a single stroke. A *determinative* (qualifying) relationship, as in работоспосо́бность, in which the first stem expresses not an attribute but another limiting factor, here an object, is denoted by a double stroke. Brackets indicate that all the elements represented by the symbols within the brackets stand in an identical lexico-grammatical relationship to the elements represented by the symbols preceding or succeeding the brackets.

The lexico-grammatical relationships existing between all-modifying affixes and the stems to which they refer are very complex and cannot easily be represented symbolically. In the formulae only the relevance of affixes is shown by the attachment to, or separation from, the symbols for stems of the symbols *p*, *s*. The function of each all-modifying affix (operating within the range of relevance indicated) is described in §8.

In every case the symbols denoting limiting (subordinate) elements are placed before those denoting limited (main) elements. The descriptions of the three examples given above therefore appear in this notation as follows:

> СССР [(*p2s+3s*)/4]//*1* (structural formulae: (precise) *1-p2s-3s-4*; (simplified) **1-2-3-4**).
> спорткружо́к *1s/2s* (*1s-2s*; **1-2**).
> работоспосо́бность *1//2s* (*1-0-2s*; **1-0-2**).

The elements of most words with abbreviated stems are linked in complex relationships. In the case of СССР we are faced with four lexico-grammatical units, each expressed by one letter only, standing in co-ordinate (*p2s+3s*), subordinate attributive (*p2s+3s*)/*4* and subordinate determinative [(*p2s+3s*)/*4*]//*1* relationships. In many cases one stem (or abbreviated stem) is the focus of two or more relationships, each of which must be described separately. In the word НТОЛеспро́м (= нау́чно-техни́ческое о́бщество лесно́й промы́шленности) the meaning of the stem -О- (= о́бщество) is restricted both by that of the attributive combination НТ- (= нау́чно-техни́ческое) and by that of the delimiting combination -Леспро́м (= лесно́й промы́шленности), and the compound must be described as

(*p1s+2s*)/*3s*, (*4s/p5ss*)//*3s*

—the comma separating, in this and similar cases, two statements in symbolic form concerning the same compound.

The deduction of formulae for words such as those consisting entirely or mostly of initials is of very little practical value to the student as the problem of relationships can only arise once the elements of a word are analysed and understood. Words of this kind are, however, included in the list in order to exemplify the double set (attributive, determinative) of subordinate relationships very frequently found in compounds with four or more stems.

There are numerous types of subordinate determinative relationship. These can be most conveniently brought together under the following headings:

(1) *Object-relationship*, as in завхóз, работоспосóбность, управдóм, when the main stem functions in the same way as a verb governing the accusative case or as a noun taking a complement in the genitive case. The subordinate stem functions like the direct object of a verb, the meaning of the main stem being delimited by the indication of the thing (or person) upon which action or potential action is directed. All but a few of the compound words with determinative subordination belong to this group.

(2) *Ethic relationship*, as in Детги́з, НТОЛеспрóм, минвнешторг. In these examples the subordinate stem (*дет*-; (-внеш-) *торг*; (Лес-)*пром*) denotes the thing or person for which or for the benefit of whom exists the thing or person expressed by the main stem. This ethic relationship may also be called 'genitive' as the noun of the main stem may be regarded as the possession of the noun of the subordinate stem. Compare the English translations *Ministry for Foreign Trade* and *Ministry of Foreign Trade*. Only compounds in which both main and subordinate stems are nominal or adjectival in origin and nominal in meaning present this relationship.

(3) *Adverbial relationship*, as in вездехóд, грязелечéние, 'mud-bath therapy'. Here the underlay or supposed underlay contains an adverb or a noun (or adjective) in the instrumental case, and the meaning of the main stem in the compound is delimited by the indication of the means with which, or the manner in which, the action denoted by that stem is performed. Very few compounds present this relationship.

(4) *Indefinite relationship*. In some cases the determinative relationship is obscure and can be described in several ways. The stems of жаропрóчный (heatproof) and огнеопáсность (inflammability), for instance, do not stand in any of the three types of relationship described above, and the lexical connection between them might best be described by the equation 1//2 = '2, as far as 1 is concerned'. There appear to be very few compounds

containing stems related in this way. They should not be confused with compounds presenting a mixture of two of the relationships described above (e.g. животво́рный, 'life-giving', in which the relationship of the subordinate to the main stem may be described either as 'adverbial' or as 'accusative').

In the table only the exceptional (ethic, adverbial, indefinite) relationships are indicated (by the abbreviations *E*, *A*, *I*, at the end of the formula).

Table 1. *Analysis of compound words*[1]

Basic structural type: **1-2**
Relationship between stems: Subordinate attributive

	A. *Stem-etymologies*	(>)	B. *Stem-functions*	C. *Structure*	D. *Relationships*
аэродинáмика	u:n		a:n	*10-2s*	*1/2s*
аэропóрт	u:n		a:n	*10-2*	*1/2*
гидроплáн	u:n		a:n	*10-2*	*1/2*
гидросамолёт	u:n		a:n	*10-p2*	*1/p2*
киноартист	u:n		a:n	*10-2s*	*1/2s*
колхóз*	a:n		a:n	*1s-2s*	*1s/2s*
Лф	a:n		a:n	*1s-2*	*1s/2*
мехчáсти	a:n		a:n	*1s-2*	*1s/2*
мотодрезина	u:n		a:n	*10-2*	*1/2*
моторóллер	u:n		a:n	*10-2*	*1/2*
НД	a:n		a:n	*p1s-2s*	*p1s/2s*
совхóз	a:n		a:n	*p1s-2s*	*p1s/2s*
спорткружóк	a:n		a:n	*1s-2s*	*1s/2s*
спорттовáры	a:n		a:n	*1s-2*	*1s/2*
телегрáф	u:u		a:n	*1-2*	*1/2*
телескóп	u:u		a:n	*1-2*	*1/2*
физóрг	a:n		a:n	*1s-2s*	*1s/2s*
фотокóпия	u:n		a:n	*10-2s*	*1/2s*
электровóз	u:u		a:n	*10-2*	*1/2*

[1] See the notes on the table, on p. 66. Forms marked * are explained at the end of the table (see p. 65).

Basic structural type: **1-2**
Relationship between stems: Subordinate determinative

	A. *Stem-etymologies*	(>)	B. *Stem-functions*	C. *Structure*	D. *Relationships*
англома́н	u:u		n:n	*10-2*	*1//2*
библио́граф	u:u		n:n	*10-2*	*1//2*
вездехо́д	adv:u		adv:n	*1-2*	*1//2A*
виноде́л	n:u		n:n	*1-2*	*1//2*
времяисчисле́ние	n:n		n:n	*1-p2s*	*1//p2s*
галлома́ния	u:n/u		n:n	*10-2s*	*1//2s*
гео́граф	u:u		n:n	*10-2*	*1//2*
германофо́б	u:u		n:n	*10-2*	*1//2*
завхо́з*	pt:n		n:n	*p1s-2s*	*2s//p1s*
русофи́л	u:u		n:n	*10-2*	*1//2*
славянофи́л	n:u		n:n	*10-2*	*1//2*
спектроско́п	u:u		n:n	*10-2*	*1//2*
управдо́м	pt:n		n:n	*p1s-2*	*2//p1s*
хроно́метр	u:u		n:n	*10-2*	*1//2*
экскурсово́д	n:u or a:u		n:n	*10-2*	*1//2*

Basic structural type: **1-2**
Relationship between stems: Co-ordinate

кни́жка-па́мятка	n:n		n:n	*1s-2s*	*1s+2s*
профе́ссорско-преподава́тельский	n:n		a:a or n:n	*1so-pp2ss*	*1s+pp2ss*

Basic structural type: **1-0-2**
Relationship between stems: Subordinate attributive

водопа́д	n:u		a:n	*1-0-2*	*1/2*
коротковоло́сый	a:n		a:n	*1-0-2*	*1/2*

маши́нопись (?)	n:u	a:n(?)	*1-0-2*	*1/2(?)*
мертворождённый	a:pt	adv:a	*1-0-2s*	*1/2s*
металлозаво́д	n:n or a:n	a:n	*1-0-p2*	*1/p2*
ржавокори́чневый	a:a	adv:a	*1-0-2s*	*1/2s*
черноволо́сый	a:n	a:n	*1-0-2*	*1/2*

Basic structural type: **1-0-2**
Relationship between stems: Subordinate determinative

винторе́з	n:u	n:n	*1-0-2*	*1//2*
водоро́д	n:u	n:n	*1-0-2*	*1//2*
жаропро́чный	n:a	n:a	*1-0-2s*	*1//2sI*
землеко́п	n:u	n:n	*1-0-2*	*1//2*
землеме́р	n:u	n:n	*1-0-2*	*1//2*
китобо́й	n:u	n:n	*1-0-2*	*1//2*
лесово́з	n:u	n:n	*1-0-2*	*1//2E*
маши́нопись (?)	n:u	n:n(?)	*1-0-2*	*1//2A(?)*
нефтепрово́д	n:u	n:n	*1-0-p2*	*1//p2E*
почвове́д	n:u	n:n	*1-0-2*	*1//2*
пулемёт	n:u	n:n	*1-0-2*	*1//2*
пылесо́с	n:u	n:n	*1-0-2*	*1//2*
работоспосо́бность	n:a	n:n	*1-0-2s*	*1//2s* or *s(1//2)*
скотово́д	n:u	n:n	*1-0-2*	*1//2*
сталева́р	n:u	n:n	*1-0-2*	*1//2*
судострои́тельный	n:a	n:a	*1-0-2ss*	*1//2s*
теплохо́д	n:u or a:u	n:n	*1-0-2*	*1//2A*
тигроло́в	n:u	n:n	*1-0-2*	*1//2*
углеро́д	n:u	n:n	*1-0-2*	*1//2*
языкове́д	n:u	n:n	*1-0-2*	*1//2*

	A. Stem-etymologies	(>)	B. Stem-functions	C. Structure	(>)	D. Relationships
Basic structural type: **1-0-2**						
Relationship between stems: Co-ordinate						
глухонемóй	a:a		a:a	*1-0-2*		*1 + 2*
Basic structural type: **1-2-s**						
Relationship between stems: Subordinate attributive						
двуствóлка	num:n		(a:n) or (num:n)	*1-2-s*		*s(1/2)*
двухимённый	num:n		(a:n) or (num:n)	*1-2-s*		*s(1/2)*
ежесýточный	a:n		(a:n)	*10-2-s*		*s(1/2)*
микроскопи́я	u:u		(a:n)	*10-2-s*		*s(1/2)*
пятиднéвный	num:n		(a:n) or (num:n)	*1-2-s*		*s(1/2)*
стереофони́я	u:u		(a:n)	*10-2-s*		*s(1/2)*
Basic structural type: **1-2-s**						
Relationship between stems: Subordinate determinative						
англофи́льство	u:u		(n:n)	*10-2-s*		*s(1//2)*
антропомéтрия	u:u		(n:n)	*10-2-s*		*s(1//2)*
маслодéлие	n:u		(n:n)	*1-2-s*		*s(1//2)*
мясорýбка	n:u		(n:n)	*1-2-s*		*s(1//2)*
юдофóбство	u:u		(n:n)	*10-2-s*		*s(1//2)*
Basic structural type: **1-0-2-s**						
Relationship between stems: Subordinate attributive						
длинновóлновый	a:n		(a:n)	*1-0-2-s*		*s(1/2)*
красноармéец	a:n		(a:n)	*1-0-2-s*		*s(1/2)*
мягкосердéчный	a:n		(a:n)	*1-0-2-s*		*s(1/2)*
низкосóртный	a:n		(a:n)	*1-0-2-s*		*s(1/2)*
однообъекти́вный	num:n		(num:n) or (a:n)	*1-0-2-s*		*s(1/2)*

Basic structural type: **1-0-2-s**
Relationship between stems: Subordinate determinative

животво́рный	adv:u or a:u	(adv:a) or (a:a)	*1-0-2-s*	*s(1//2A) (?)*
зверoло́вство	n:u	(n:n)	*1-0-2-s*	*s(1//2)*
плодоро́дный	n:u	(n:?)	*1-0-2-s*	*s(1//2)*
пчеловóдство	n:u	(n:n)	*1-0-2-s*	*s(1//2)*
скотобóйня	n:u	(n:n)	*1-0-2-s*	*s(1//2)*
счетовóдство	n:u	(n:?)	*1-0-2-s*	*s(1//2)*
языкове́дение	n:u	(n:n)	*1-0-2-s*	*s(1//2)*

Basic structural type: **1-0-2-s**
Relationship between stems: Co-ordinate

товáро-пассажи́рский	n:n	(n:n)	*1-0-2-s*	*s(1+2)*

Basic structural type: **1-2-3**
Primary relationship between stems: Subordinate attributive

вуз*	a:a:n	a:a:n	*1s-2s-p3s*	*1s/(2s/p3s)*
Детги́з	n:a:n or a:a:n	n:a:n or a:a:n	*1s?-2ss-p3ss*	*(1s+2ss)/p3ss* or *1s//(2ss/p3ss) E*
дормехбáза	n:a:n	a:a:n	*1s?-2s-3*	*(1s+2s)/3*
ЗИЛ	n:n:n	n:?:?	*p1-2-3*	*(3//2)/p1*
РÓСТА	n:a:n	a:a:n	*1s-2s-3s*	*1s/(2s/3s)*

	A. *Stem-etymologies* (>)	**B.** *Stem-functions*	**C.** *Structure* (>)	**D.** *Relationships*
Basic structural type: **1-2-3**				
Primary relationship between stems: Subordinate determinative				
минвнешто́рг	n:a:n	n:a:n	*1s-2s-3s*	*(2s/3s)//1sE*
предколхо́з	n:a:n	n:a:n	*p1s-2s-3s*	*(2s/3s)//p1s*
Basic structural type: **1-2-3**				
Primary relationships between stems: Subordinate attributive and subordinate determinative				
Ленавтоуправле́ние*	a:a:n	a:a:n	*1s?-2s-p3s*	*1s/p3s, 2s//p3s*
Basic structural type: **1-2-3-4**				
Primary relationship between stems: Subordinate attributive				
главсельстройпрое́кт	a:a:a:n or a:a:n:n	a:a:n:n	*1s?-2s?-3s?-4s?*	*2/(3/4/1)* (simplified)
КПСС*	a:n:a:n	a:n:a:n	*1ss-2-p3s-4*	*(3/4)/(1/2)* (simplified)
ТАСС	a:n:a:n	a:n:a:n	*1s-2s-p3s-4*	*(3/4)/(1/2)* (simplified)
Basic structural type: **1-2-3-4**				
Primary relationship between stems: Subordinate determinative				
СССР	n:a:a:n	n:a:a:n	*1-p2s-3s-4*	*[(2+3)/4]//1* (simplified)
Basic structural type: **1-2-3-4**				
Primary relationships between stems: Subordinate attributive and subordinate determinative				
МПВП	a:a:n:n	a:a:n:n	*pp1s-p2s-p3s-p4*	*(1+2)/3, 4//3* (simplified)
облоно́*	a:n:a:n	a:n:a:n	*p1s-p2-p3s-p4s*	*1/2, (3/4)//2E* (simplified)

Basic structural type: **1-2-3-4-5**
Primary relationships between stems: Subordinate attributive and subordinate determinative

ЛОНТÓ	a:a:a:a:n	a:n:a:a:n	*1s-p2s-p3s-4s-5s*	*1/2*, [(*3+4*)/*5*]//*2* (simplified)
НИИТеплоприбóр	a:a:n:a:n	a:a:n:a:n	*p1s-p2ss-3-405s-p607s*	(*1+2*)/*3*, (*4/6*)//*3E* (simplified)
НТОЛеспрóм	a:a:n:a:a	a:a:n:a:n	*p1s-2s-3s-4s-p5ss*	(*1+2*)/*3*, (*4/5*)//*3E* (simplified)

Basic structural type: **1-2-3-4-5-6**
Primary relationships between stems: Subordinate attributive and subordinate determinative

НТОНГП	a:a:n:a:a:a	a:a:n:a:a:n	*p1s-2s-3s-4s-5s-p6ss*	(*1+2*)/*3*, [(*4+5*)/*6*]//*3E* (simplified)

Basic structural type: **p-1-0-2-s**
Primary relationship between stems: Subordinate determinative

неплодорóдность	n:u	(n:-)	*p-1-0-2-s*	*p*[*s*(*1//2*)] or *s*[*p*(*1//2*)]

вуз	вы́сшее учéбное заведéние (Institute of Higher Education)
завхóз	завéдующий хозя́йством (a manager)
колхóз	коллекти́вное хозя́йство (a collective farm)
КПСС	Коммунисти́ческая Пáртия Совéтского Сою́за (the Communist Party of the Soviet Union)
Ленавтоуправлéние	Ленингрáдское управлéние автотрáнспортом (Leningrad Transport Administration)
облонó	областнóй отдéл нарóдного образовáния (a regional department of education)

Notes on Table 1

1. Nearly all two-stem compounds in Russian are regressive: the first stem modifies or qualifies the second, the second stem governs the first. Exceptions are rare (here завхо́з, управдо́м only). Many of the compounds with three or four stems which present only one primary relationship (here зил, минвнешто́рг, предколхо́з, КПСС, ТАСС, СССР) are, however, progressive. This is probably because they are contractions of phrases with progressive syntax.

2. The table does not indicate the frequency of occurrence of the three types of relationship. In practice it will be found that the two kinds of subordinate relationship are equally common, and that the co-ordinate relationship is rare, in the two-stem compounds.

3. In two-stem compounds stems joined in the subordinate attributive relationship usually function as adjective and noun. In origin the first stem is normally a or u and the second stem is normally n or u. Stems in a subordinate determinative relationship usually function as two nouns. In nearly all cases both stems are n or u in origin. Stems in the co-ordinate relationship have identical functions which may be either nominal or adjectival as determined by their origins. Exceptions to these general rules should be noted from the table.

4. In compounds with three or more stems it is important to seek the primary relationship(s) between the stems in order to avoid confusion. The distinction between primary and secondary relationships in the examples given is shown in the Relationships formula, where symbols denoting secondary relationship are enclosed in brackets.

5. In three-stem compounds stems in a primarily subordinate attributive relationship usually function as adjective-adjective-noun. Where the primary relationship is subordinate determinative the stems normally function as noun-adjective-noun.

6. In three- and four-stem compounds the subordinate attributive is the most common primary relationship. Where two sets of relationships occur (as in many compounds with three or more stems) one is primarily subordinate attributive and the other primarily subordinate determinative.

7. In compounds with an all-modifying suffix (basic types **1-2-s**, **1-0-2-s**, **p-1-0-2-s**) there is no close correlation between the function of the suffix (nominal, adjectival) and the relationship between the stems of the word.

8. The presence of a link-vowel is not a factor determining or influencing the relationship between the stems which it joins.

6

WORD-FORMATION IN RUSSIAN: AN HISTORICAL OUTLINE

It is convenient to divide an historical review of word formation in literary Russian into six sections, each of which corresponds to an historical period characterized by the prominence of certain procedures and, more especially, by the prominence of certain types of material used in these procedures. No attempt can be made here to give any but the barest outline of the growth of the present system of word formation, but it is hoped that this will be enough to show which procedures have been consistently popular (e.g. borrowing, suffixation) and which have only recently become highly productive (e.g. compounding with abbreviated components, shortening).

The second to sixth of the historical periods begin with the separation of Russian from East Slavonic (that is, from a literary language showing few features specific to the Russian, Ukrainian and Belorussian languages of which it was the ancestor) which becomes apparent in fourteenth-century texts. These last five periods may be given names to indicate the chief immediate sources from which words were taken into Russian, the adaptation of these words to the morphological and phonetic norms of the language being the most striking feature of each period. The fourteenth and fifteenth centuries (the Greek and Turkic period) were a time of relatively slow lexical change. The sixteenth and seventeenth centuries (the Latin and Polish period) were dominated linguistically by the development of heavy bureaucratic and epistolary styles. The eighteenth and early nineteenth centuries (the German and French period) saw the acceptance of Western European literary genres, the century preceding the Revolution of 1917 (the French and International period) was one of remarkable intellectual and technical progress in which the vocabulary of the language was possibly doubled in size. The years since 1917 (the English and International period) are without parallel in the rate of expansion in word formation, an expansion demanded by great political, social and scientific changes and brought about largely by the use of techniques only poorly exploited in the pre-Revolutionary period.

There are a number of morphological features by which purely Russian words (of any period) can be distinguished from those in use in Common or East Slavonic. Words in the following categories date from a period later than the separation of Russian from East Slavonic (the fourteenth century).

1. Most nouns with the suffix -тель denoting instruments, e.g. выключа́тель (a switch).
2. Most nouns with the suffix -ость with foreign roots, e.g. автоно́мность (autonomy).
3. Nearly all adjectives with the suffixes -ч-ат-, -чив-, e.g. перели́вчатый (iridescent), заду́мчивый (pensive).
4. All nouns with the suffixes -л-к-а, -ов-к-а, -ов-щик, -тель-ств-о, -чик/-щик, -чин-а/-щин-а, -ш-а, -ят-ин-а, e.g. гада́лка (a fortune-teller), листо́вка (a leaflet), фруктовщи́к (a seller of fruit), прави́тельство (a government), счётчик (a meter), ба́рщина (a work-duty), генера́льша (a general's wife), порося́тина (young pork).
5. All adjectives with imported prefixes and Russian roots, e.g. архиплу́т (a great scoundrel).
6. Nearly all deaffixed deverbal nouns in which the root-vowel remains unchanged, e.g. зажи́м (suppression).
7. All compound words with abbreviated stems, e.g. вуз.
8. Nearly all compound words of which at least one element is of foreign origin, e.g. центробе́жный (centrifugal).
9. All compound words with co-ordinate syntactic relationships, e.g. кни́жка-па́мятка (a memo-book).
10. Nearly all compound adjectives, e.g. работоспосо́бный (efficient).

It should be pointed out that most word-building procedures were in use both before and after the separation of Russian and that most prefixes and suffixes now in use were extant before the fourteenth century.

The earlier periods distinguished above present little of interest apart from the sources of borrowed words. Calquing was as common as direct borrowing, but compound words only were translated in this way. Земледе́лие is a seventeenth-century adaptation of Latin *agricultura*.

The eighteenth century was marked by the earliest regular use of morphemes other than roots in calques, as in Kantemir's пло́тн-ость (from Fr. *solid-ité*) and in со-стоя́ть (from Ger. *bestehen*). From this time onward there was a very great increase in the number of affixed words in Russian, among which were many with imported prefixes. Some of these became so productive that they displaced native affixes of similar meaning (as антинаро́дный has replaced противонаро́дный). On the other hand, the work of Karamzin and his supporters increased the number of native affixes in use in the literary language by the introduction of words taken from the vernacular. The development of compounding (composition) owes much to the language of the heroic and pre-romantic poetry of this and the following period, in which *ad hoc* creations such as огнекры́латый змий (Rayevsky) were common.

The nineteenth century saw a considerable development in calquing which was largely the work of Pushkin and Belinsky. Throughout this and the following period a small number of affixes were used frequently for this purpose. International *-ia* (Latin *-ia*, Greek *-eia*) was replaced by -ен-ие, -ств-о. International *-itia* (French *-ité*, English *-ity*, German *-ität*) was replaced by -ость. Half-calques came into vogue halfway through the century, a foreign root remaining untranslated but a foreign affix being replaced. Thus Belinsky (1841) used гума́нн-ость as equivalent to Ger. *Human-ität* in preference to the older челове́чн-ость.

The period 1830–60 saw the importation of a considerable number of words, chiefly of abstract meaning, from German. These words were nearly all compound and were translated as such in Russian: *augenscheinlich* became очеви́дный for instance. These and other words taken from German (e.g. *Vorstellung*/представле́ние) were rarely borrowed directly as was the case with words taken from English or French, which often contained morphemes recognizable as International.

The enormous linguistic changes accompanying the development of Soviet Russia after 1917 were to some small extent foreshadowed by innovations dating from the early years of this century. A few nouns were formed by joining together abbreviated stems, as in военми́н (Ministry of War), ЦК (цэка́ = 'Central Committee'), and the first Russian words created 'from nothing' began to circulate shortly before the First World War in the poems of Bely and Khlebnikov. The Revolution and its aftermath led to a period of very rapid social and technological change, change that was reflected clearly in the Russian language. And nowhere were developments more profound than in the lexicon, the category most sensitive to change in any language. New words were needed to denote the political, social and administrative institutions of a society which was to be almost completely rebuilt, and it is words with these functions that provide the bulk of the lexicon created since 1917. Not only are recently created words numerous, making up not less than a quarter of the whole vocabulary of Russian, but many of them are of very frequent occurrence. According to the most recently published word frequency count (Shteinfeldt, 1963) the new forms колхóз, комсóмольский, комсомóлец, комсомóл, and the polysemanticized товáрищ, совéтский, пионéр, бригáда, совéт, пáртия, пионéрский, are among the three hundred words most common in literary Russian, being used more often than, for example, скóро, приéхать, лýчший or сын.

Lexical development since 1917 comprises on the one hand the creation of many thousands of neologisms, very many of which have been absorbed into the active vocabulary, an increase in polysemanticization and an increase in the size of the stylistically neutral vocabulary, and on the other the passing of some older words into the passive vocabulary, some desemanticization and the shrinking of stylistically specialized vocabularies. Of these developments the formation of neologisms by affixation, compounding or borrowing (with varying degrees of adaptation to the phonological norms of the language) greatly outweighs in importance all other changes. Polysemanticization is seen in the words кустáрный (in the sense of 'primitive'), пионéр (in the sense of 'member of a youth organization'), and учáсток (in the sense of 'sphere of social activity') and in a few dozen others. A very few words are for the most part now used passively (are recognized) only, e.g. гимнáзия, трактúр, царь, and even fewer words have undergone a perceptible loss of meaning, e.g. манкúровать, which has been replaced in two of its three basic senses by пренебрегáть.

The neologisms which have won acceptance since 1917 are words built according to morphological principles established before the Revolution, however poorly these may previously have been illustrated. Attempts to depart from these principles such as those seen in the arbitrary creations of Ivanov, who imitated the phonetic groups of Kirgiz, of Kryuchonykh, who tried to use as often as possible the letters occurring toward the end of the Russian alphabet, or of Leonov, who tried to introduce words beginning with ы, have not had lasting effects.

The following formal means have been in common use since the Revolution:

1. Suffixation, especially with the morphemes -ен-ие, -ик, -ист, -чик/-щик as in прилунле́ние (moonfall), кадрови́к (a member of a cadre), трактори́ст (a tractor driver), нефтепрово́дчик (a worker on a pipe-line). All these suffixes have been in use for centuries.

2. Compounding with abbreviated stems, as in агитпу́нкт (a propaganda centre), НЭП (New Economic Policy). The earliest words of this type date from about 1890.

3. Compounding with whole stems. The co-ordinate relationship between the stems is especially characteristic of post-Revolutionary words, e.g. нау́чно-иссле́довательский (scientific research), тури́ст-иностра́нец (a foreign tourist).

4. Compounding by the telescoping of a phrase, most often with the addition of the suffix -к-а, as in тушёнка (stewed meat), from тушёное мя́со. Both this and the preceding procedure were in limited use during the nineteenth century.

5. The adaptation to Russian norms of borrowed words. Nearly all of the words composing the specialized and popular vocabularies of chemistry, physics, and, to a lesser degree, biology, are built up from International roots and affixes and it is impossible to say, without extra information, from which languages words such as аэродина́мика, киберне́тика, микрокли́мат and гибридиза́ция are taken. Where roots other than those of the International vocabulary are used (as in джаз, корнфле́йксы, джи́нсы), the phonetic shape of the borrowed word usually indicates its origin. The form *жаз, would suggest that the word *jazz* had been borrowed through French.

The developments in vocabulary since 1917 presented both positive and negative features. While the most highly exploited procedure (compounding with abbreviated stems) has afforded great concision and economy by the reduction of whole words, or even phrases, to single syllables, the over-enthusiastic use of abbreviation has often led to a breakdown in communication. While some abbreviations, felt to be urgently needed by a large number of speakers, have become common linguistic property (e.g. вуз, мосгорсове́т), the majority of contracted words or phrases have never acquired currency outside jargons.

7

CONCLUSIONS

In comparing procedures used in English and Russian to form nouns and adjectives we see that similarities greatly outweigh differences. Speakers of both languages use affixation and composition according to the structural patterns and ranges of applicability determined by a usage which allows very great liberty in both respects. In both languages there is an enormous reservoir of 'potential words', any of which may be brought into existence by combining morphemes in an approved way. In both languages polysemanticization is proceeding rapidly and almost unobserved in response to a desire for generalization that is also reflected in a levelling of literary styles. The need for economy in the transmission of information regarding complex objects and institutions has led, in English and (to an even greater extent) in Russian, to the frequent abbreviation of words and phrases.

The two languages differ in their word-forming procedures only in that Russian speakers do not use reduplication of meaningful syllables, and the creation of words 'from nothing' is not tolerated in the literary language. Of the remaining eleven procedures the reduplication of meaningless syllables and resemanticization cannot be observed in either language, yet there is no reason to believe that these have become unproductive. Internal modification is still practised in the Russian verb system but is not used in the formation of nouns or adjectives and is quite unproductive in English. The other methods (borrowing of words and morphemes, polysemanticization, affixation, compounding, etc.) are all in use in both English and Russian, although to varying degrees. Words from the International vocabulary enter both languages freely and calques are rarely formed. Generalization of meaning has become almost as common in Russian as it is in English, although the appearance of a word with a new extension of meaning in the former language does not pass unnoticed as in the latter, and such words are always written for a time within quotation marks. Change of grammatical class and stress-shift are rare in Russian, but are not uncommon in English.

Affixation and compounding are the most active procedures in both languages. Curiously enough, the first of these is used almost without restraint in English, where such words as *tenderization*, *re-entrant*, *discounting* are accepted without question, but Russian speakers are reluctant to form new affixed words unless they serve to replace very unwieldy phrases. On the other hand, far fewer compound words are created in English than in Russian, probably because the telescoping of phrases into compounds with abbreviated stems is rendered unnecessary by the grammatical possibilities of English and the shortness of words in that language.

Familiarity with these commonly used procedures is of very great value to the foreign student of either language. The existence of these (and other) formal derivatory processes means that only a small proportion of the words of either English or Russian needs to be actively memorized in order to provide a wide recognition vocabulary. Even more important from the student's point of view is the fact that a sound knowledge of the functions of the morphemes used in affixation and compounding can compensate for many deficiencies in the student's stock of words for active use in speaking or writing.

8

THE MOST COMMONLY USED AFFIXES

It is intended to give in this section as full a description of the commoner prefixes and suffixes as space permits. The aim of this description, and of the choice of affixes to be described, is frankly utilitarian.

Only affixes that are both productive (P or VP) and of frequent occurrence (being found in at least fifty words) have been included. It is recommended for practical purposes that the lexico-grammatical, phonetic and intonational functions of each of the affixes listed below be understood and that the examples given be memorized. Practice in creating 'potential words' from known stems with the help of one (or more) of these affixes, confirming the existence of such words (where this is the case) by looking them up in a dictionary, should be found well worth while.

Fifteen prefixes and thirty suffixes are listed, in alphabetical order. Prefixes used in deverbal forms are excluded because they are not combined immediately with stems to form either nouns or adjectives.

The description of each affix covers its productiveness in each of its lexical functions, its phonetic functions (whether or not it causes softening or mutation), its intonational functions (whether or not it causes displacement of stress), and its lexico-grammatical function or functions. Affixes precisely or nearly synonymous or antonymous to the given affix are listed. One example of the use of the affix in each of its lexical functions is given, these examples being contained in phrases (taken from contemporary literature or from the largest modern dictionaries) to facilitate memorizing.

Prefixes are distinguished in the initial entry by the absence of a preceding hyphen (as in авто-), noun suffixes by the absence of a following hyphen (as in -аж) and adjective suffixes by the presence of hyphens in both positions (as in -енн-). Variant forms distinguished phonetically but of identical functions are given in brackets, e.g. без- (безъ-, бес-). In order to avoid repetition of information, no compound affixes are listed in §8. To discover the functions of any of these affixes the affix should be sought in §9. Each of its productive and lexically meaningful components may then be looked up in §8. Thus the meaning of -тельство (as in прави́тельство), listed under -ств-о in §9 as -тель⁰-ств-о, may be ascertained by looking up -ств-о *alone* in §8. This is because -тель may be regarded as meaningless in the given compound suffix.

Numerals in square brackets indicate the number of words in which the given affix is found according to Ozhegov and Shapiro and Bielfeldt. See further the remarks on p. 90.

The abbreviations used are as follows:

Prod: *Degree of productiveness* possessed by the affix in each of its lexical or lexico-grammatical functions. VP indicates that the affix is in frequent use (and that the student may use it with confidence in word-building). P indicates that the affix is used to form a considerable number of new words (and that it may be used actively by the student if care is taken to attach it only to stems of the lexical and grammatical type to which it is most commonly applicable). WP indicates that the affix in the given meaning is now used only rarely; NP indicates that it is completely dead. No affixes in these categories should be used in attempts to form words.

App: *Applicability*. This denotes the type of stems with which an affix may be used, 'type' relating to the grammatical category of the word or words from which the stem is taken.

Mut: *Mutation*. In the case of suffixes causing mutation of (final) stem-consonants a list of the consonants affected is given and the change occurring in each case indicated.

Soft: *Softening*. In the case of suffixes causing softening the word 'All' here indicates that any stem-consonant capable of softening is affected in this way by the suffix in question. Softening of some consonants only is noted here also.

Str: *Change of stress position*. This is noted where the addition of an affix frequently causes the main stress to move off one of the syllables of the stems on to another, or on to the affix or part of the affix. 'Forward' denotes movement of stress toward *the initial syllable* of a word.

Lex: *Lexical function* of the affix, expressed either descriptively (e.g. 'Intensity', this being a quality found in the affixed word but not in the stem previous to affixation) or by the quoting of English affixes of similar meaning.

Syn and Ant: Here are noted affixes of *similar or opposite lexical function.* Where congruence is quite or very nearly complete the sign = (equivalent to) is used before the affixes. Where the affixes mentioned are synonymous or antonymous only in certain contexts or in combination with certain stems, the sign ≃ (approximately equivalent to) is used. This information is given only to aid learning by comparison and it should not be thought that synonymous affixes are interchangeable.

N.B.: *A special note* on phonetic, lexical or grammatical functions of the affix or on the association of the affix with other affixes in derived words.

АВТО- [200+]

Prod: P.

App: Nouns and adjectives, nearly all of which are of foreign origin.

Lex: 'Self-, auto-'.

Syn: = сам-о-.

Example: Автобиографи́ческий элеме́нт рома́на (the autobiographical element in a novel). Cf. биогра́фия, 'a biography'.

-АЖ [70+]

Prod: (1) P. (2) NP.

App: (1) Stems of nouns and verbs of foreign origin. Forms with native stems, e.g. подхалима́ж (boot-licking), are not considered literary.
(2) Stems of nouns and adjectives of foreign and (rarely) of native origin.

Str: Backward on to the suffix. In oblique cases the stress falls on the termination.

Lex: (1) Actions.
(2) Objects.

Syn: (1) ≃ -ств-о.

Examples: (1) Пилота́ж по прибо́рам (flying by instruments). Cf. пило́т, 'a pilot'.
(2) Репорта́ж о футбо́льном ма́тче (a football commentary). Cf. репортёр, 'a reporter'.

-АНТ (-ЯНТ) [100+]

Prod: P.

App: Stems of nouns. Stems of verbs of foreign origin in -ировать, which is replaced by -ант.

Lex: Persons characterized by association with objects (as in курса́нт) or by actions (as in эмигра́нт), '-er, -ent, -ant, -é, -ee'.

Syn: ≃ -ент.

N.B.: -ант is found as an unperceived suffix in many borrowed words (e.g. дилета́нт, 'a dilettante') which serve as bases for other suffixed forms (e.g. дилета́нтка, дилета́нтство).

Example: Сейча́с ведёт экскурса́нтов по го́роду (he's taking some trippers round the town at the moment). Cf. экску́рсия, 'a trip'.

АНТИ- [120+]

Prod: P.

App: Adjectives and, less commonly, nouns, nearly all of which are of foreign origin.

Lex: 'anti-'.
Syn: = противо-, ≃ контр-.
Ant: = про-.
Example: Антиобщéственный постýпок (an anti-social act). Cf. óбщество, 'society'.

БЕЗ- (БЕЗЪ-, БЕС-) [450+/25+]
Prod: (1) VP. (2) WP.
App: (1) Nouns and adjectives and (2) nouns, nearly all of which are of native origin.
Lex: (1) Negation. (2) Absence of an object.
Syn: (1) ≃ а-.
Ant: (1) ≃ не-без-.
N.B.: Initial и is replaced by ы after без-. In adjectives без- is nearly always used with the suffix -н-.
Examples: (1) Беззастéнчивая ложь (a barefaced lie). Cf. застéнчивый, 'timid'.
(2) Безбилéтный пассажи́р (a stowaway). Cf. билéт, 'a ticket'.

ДЕ- (ДЕЗ-) [200+]
Prod: P.
App: Nouns, all of which are of foreign origin.
Lex: Reversal of action, 'de-, dis-'.
Syn: ≃ раз- (verbal).
N.B.: There are a few exceptions to the rule that де- is used before a consonant, дез- before a vowel: деавтоматизáция, 'de-automation'; деаэрáтор, 'a de-aerator'; деаэрáция, 'de-aeration' (of water); деэмульсáтор, 'a de-emulsifier'; деэмульсáция, 'de-emulsification'; деэтимологизáция, 'de-etymologization'.
Example: Дезинфéкция произвóдится у нас хлóром (we use chlorine as a disinfectant). Cf. инфéкция, 'infection'.

-ЕНН- (-ЯНН-) [70+/150+]
Prod: (1) P. (2) NP.
App: (1) Stems of nouns with the suffix -ств-о. Older forms are derived from nouns with the suffixes -знь, -изн-а and the final syllables -ва, -во (e.g. жизнь; укори́зна, 'a reproach'; листвá, 'foliage, yield'; дéрево, 'a tree': жи́зненный, 'vital'; безукори́зненный, 'irreproachable'; ли́ственный, 'deciduous'; деревя́нный, 'wooden').
(2) Stems of adjectives (rare).
Soft: All.
Lex: (1) Related to an object. The idea of quality often proceeds from this.
(2) Intensified, 'very' (rare).
Syn: (1) ≃ -ск-.
N.B.: Formally identical with one of the varieties of the suffix -нн-, -енн-, which is found in the past passive participles of many verbs in -ить and in adjectives which have developed from these participles. See -НН-.
Examples: (1) Клю́квенный сок (cranberry juice). Cf. клю́ква, 'cranberries'.
(2) Здоровéнный пáрень (a very fit young man). Cf. здорóвый, 'healthy'.

-ЕЦ [600+/230+]

Prod: (1) (2) VP. (3) (4) (5) NP. (Others) NP.

App: (1) Stems of nouns denoting places.
(2) Stems of nouns. Deverbal nouns in -ен-ие frequently serve as words of origin.
(3) Infinitive stems of verbs (with the suffix of the past passive participle).
(4) Infinitive stems of verbs. The past tense form of verbs, as in пришéлец (a new arrival).
(5) Infinitive stems of verbs.
(Others) Various. Stems of adjectives are most common.

Soft: All.

Str: Generally, no change. Derived words with monosyllabic stems may have the stress on the suffix: in these nouns the stress is final throughout (e.g. the gen. sing. of жилéц, 'an inhabitant', is жильцá).

Lex: (1) Persons characterized by the place of their birth or residence, '-an, -er'.
(2) Persons characterized by membership of an organization or by connection with a movement.
(3) Persons characterized by experience undergone.
(4) Persons characterized by action performed.
(5) Instruments.
(Others) The suffix -ец is used with a number of stems, most of which are adjectival in origin, to form nouns denoting a very wide variety of objects. The function of the suffix in nouns such as вдовéц (a widower), румя́нец (a blush), самéц (a male animal), appears to be almost purely grammatical.

Syn: (1) = -ан-ин.
(2) ≃ -ник.
(4) = -ент.
(5) ≃ -ник.

N.B.: The suffix is frequently found with interfixes (lexically void affixes), as in the groups -ан-ец (америкáнец), -иан-ец (кантиáнец), -ин-ец (бáкинец), -ов-ец (исполкомóвец). These groups may be regarded for practical purposes as compound affixes, and are listed as such.

Examples: (1) Украи́нцы — оди́н из трёх востóчно-славя́нских нарóдов (the Ukrainians are one of the three East Slav peoples). Cf. Украи́на, 'the Ukraine'.
(2) В 1793 г. якоби́нцы осуществи́ли диктату́ру (in 1793 the Jacobins formed a dictatorship). Cf. Я́коб, Я́ков, 'Jacob'.
(3) Урожéнец Ленингрáда (a native of Leningrad). Cf. роди́ться, 'to be born'.
(4) Снабжéнцы спрáвились образцóво (the supply organizations coped excellently). Cf. снабжáть, 'to supply'.
(5) Сáхарные щипцы́ (sugar tongs). Cf. щипáть, 'to pinch'.

-ИЗМ [300+/130+]

Prod: P.

App: Stems of nouns also found with the suffixes -ик or -ист. These are nearly all of foreign origin.

Soft: All.

Lex: Doctrines, attitudes, schools of thought, activities.
Syn: ≃ -ств-о (especially -иан-ств-о, -ов-ств-о).
Example: Его́ филосо́фия отлича́ется прагмати́змом (his philosophy is distinguished by its pragmatism). Cf. прагмати́ст.

-ИК [300+/120+]

Prod: (1) (2) P. (3) (4) WP. (5) NP.
App: (1) Stems of adjectives in -н-, -ов-, and of nouns in -изм, -ия.
(2) Stems of adjectives in -н- and of nouns in -ня.
(3) Infinitive stems of verbs with suffix of past passive participle.
(4) Stems of adjectives.
(5) Stems of numerals.
Soft: All.
Str: As a rule, no change. Where the stress in the word of origin is final as in the adjective грузово́й (cargo), the stress in the derived word is also final and remains so throughout the paradigm, as in грузови́к (a lorry, truck), nom. pl. грузовики́, gen. pl. грузовико́в.
Lex: (1) Male persons characterized by occupation or social grouping.
(2) Male persons characterized by attitude to or connection with an institution or idea.
(3) Male persons characterized by an experience undergone.
(4) Objects characterized by a single feature or by association with other objects.
(5) Objects characterized by divisibility (very rare), e.g. четвери́к, 'a team of four horses'.
Syn: (1) ≃ -ёр, -ник, -тор, -щик.
(2) (3) (4) ≃ -ник.
(4) ≃ -ов-к-а.
N.B.: Derived words with the suffix -ик with meaning (1) may be formed from the stems of adjectives or nouns. In the former case, however, the derived word always represents a phrase containing the adjective of origin, e.g. вечёрник is equivalent to студе́нт вечёрнего ку́рса ву́за. The suffixes -ник, -щик (and -чик), are etymologically related to -ик. Alternative analyses are possible in nouns derived from adjectives in -н- where these are in turn taken from other nouns: зубн-и́к or зуб-ни́к, вечёрн-ик or вечёр-ник seem equally plausible divisions.
Examples: (1) Массовики́ веду́т акти́вную агита́цию (the workers among the masses are carrying out a lively propaganda campaign). Cf. ма́ссовый, 'mass'; ма́ссы, 'the masses'.
(2) Он бездо́мник — кочу́ет по родны́м (he's never at home because he wanders from one relative to another). Cf. бездо́мный, 'homeless'.
(3) Посла́нника не принима́ли (the ambassador was not received). Cf. посла́ть, 'to send'.
(4) Фильм «Война́ и Мир» наве́рно бу́дет боевико́м (the film 'War and Peace' will almost certainly be a hit). Cf. боево́й, 'fighting, spirited'; бой, 'a battle'.

-ИН[1] (-ЫН) [250+/50+]

Prod: (1) P. (2) (3) NP.
App: (1) (2) (3) Stems of nouns usually denoting persons or animals.
Str: (1) (2) (3) No change. Where the noun of origin ends in a stressed vowel

in all cases, as in Сатана́ (Satan), the stress in the derived adjective or noun is on the suffix (here: сатани́н).

Lex: (1) Possession, ''s' (adjectives).
(2) Surnames (nouns).
(3) Names of nationalities.

N.B.: Nouns and adjectives in -ин[1], like those in -ов[1], are of irregular (mixed) declension. The suffix in тата́рин (a Tartar) is now unproductive, although it is still used in combination with interfixes, as in юж-а́н-ин (a southerner) (P), ростов-ч-а́н-ин (a man from Rostov) (WP). Note the use of -ин (-ин[3]) to translate the International suffix -in(e) in names of organic chemical compounds such as *pancreatin*, *antipyrine* (Rus. панкреа́тин, антипири́н). This suffix is weakly productive and its use is restricted to jargons.

Examples: (1) Ла́сточкино гнездо́ (the swallow's nest). Cf. ла́сточка, 'a swallow'.
(2) «Ле́нин» — подпо́льное и́мя В. И. Улья́нова (Lenin was the conspiratorial name of V. I. Ul'yanov). Cf. Ле́на, 'the river Lena'.
(3) Незва́ный гость ху́же тата́рина (an uninvited visitor is worse than a Tatar). Cf. тата́ры, 'Tatars'.

-ИН-А [350+/60+]

Prod: (1) P. (2) (3) WP. (4) NP.

App: (1) (2) Stems of nouns.
(3A) Present stems of verbs.
(3B) Infinitive stems of transitive verbs with the suffix of the past passive participle.
(4) Stems of adjectives.

Mut: к > ч, г > ж, х > ш, occasionally д > ж (in 2), ст > щ (in 4).

Soft: All.

Str: (1) (2) Change rare except in cases where the noun of origin has mobile stress. In such cases the stress in the derived word moves backward on to the и of the suffix, as in осетри́на, 'sturgeon' (the dish).
(3A) Remains on or moves to final syllable of the stem, as in изги́бина (a bend). Exceptions are морщи́на (a wrinkle) and nouns with the prefix вы-, e.g. вы́боина (a dent).
(3B) Backward to и of the suffix.
(4) Backward to a of the suffix. In the plural forms of the derived word the stress moves forward one syllable, as in глуби́ны (depths).

Lex: (1) Singulative or partitive meaning in contrast to that of the noun of origin, e.g. виногра́д (grapes), виногра́дина (a grape).
(2) Foods made from the animals or fish denoted by the nouns of origin.
(3) Objects resulting from actions.
(4) Abstract nouns, qualities.

Syn: (2) = -ят-ин-а.
(4) = -изн-а, ≃ -ость, -ье.

N.B.: This suffix is frequently used in uneducated speech to form nouns denoting objects, such as ра́дужина (also ра́дужка), 'the iris' (of an eye) (= ра́дужная оболо́чка). In this very general sense the suffix is synonymous with -ов-ин-а and like this latter has been applied to both noun and adjective stems. Do not confuse with the augmentative suffix -ин-а as in звери́на (a huge beast).

Examples: (1) Пропáла жемчýжина из э́того ожерéлья (one of the pearls is missing from this necklace). Cf. жéмчуг, 'pearls'.

(2) Котлéта из барáнины (a mutton cutlet). Cf. барáн, 'a ram, sheep'.

(3) Мы перешли́ ручéй по переклáдине (we crossed the stream by a plank thrown across it). Cf. класть, 'to lay'.

(4) Соблюдáйте тишинý (silence is to be observed). Cf. ти́хий, 'silent'.

-ИСТ[1] [300+/80+]

Prod: P.

App: Stems of nouns which may be suffixed (usually with -изм), this suffix being lost when -ист is added, as in коммуни́ст.

Soft: All.

Lex: Male persons associated with objects, institutions or ideas denoted by the nouns of origin.

Example: Романи́сты серéбряного вéка (novelists of the Silver Age). Cf. ромáн, 'a novel'.

-ИСТ[2]- [240+/10+]

Prod: (1) VP. (2) P.

App: (1) Stems of nouns (which may be combined with one of the suffixes -ан-, -н-, -ов-, as in серни́стый, 'sulphurous', from сéра).

(2) Stems of verbs and (uncommonly) of adjectives. These stems are in all cases prefixed.

Soft: All.

Str: (1) Various. Where noun of origin has final or mobile stress the stress in the derived word is on the suffix, as in волокни́стый (fibrous). Otherwise there is no change.

Lex: (1) 'Similar to' or 'characterized by' the object denoted by the stem, '-ous, -y'.

(2) 'Tending to' behave in the manner indicated by the stem, '-ous, -y'.

Syn: (1) (2) ≃ -лив-, -чив-, -яв-.

Examples: (1) Холми́стый пейзáж (a hilly landscape). Cf. холм, 'a hill'.

(2) Изги́бистая рекá (a winding river). Cf. изгибáться, 'to twist, bend'.

-К-А [3700+/1100+]

Prod: (1) VP. (2) (3) (4) (5) P. (6) (7) NP.

App: (1) Stems of masculine nouns which may be either simple or derived (already suffixed). The suffixes -ец, -ик, -ин, are lost when -к-а is added.

(2) Infinitive stems of verbs.

(3) Stems of adjectives and of past passive participles.

(4) (5) Infinitive stems of verbs.

(6) Stems of verbs, nouns, adjectives.

(7) Stems of verbs, adjectives.

Mut: к > ч, г > ж, х > ш.

Lex: (1) Female equivalent to the male persons denoted by the stems.

(2) Objects created by actions.

(3) Objects characterized by their origins, by the material from which they are made.

(4) Processes, actions.
(5) Instruments.
(6) Names (including proper names) of animals.
(7) Male or female persons characterized by habitual actions or by qualities.

Syn: (1) ≃ -их-а, -ниц-а, -ш-а, -щиц-а.
(2) ≃ -ен-ие.
(3) ≃ -ов-к-а.
(4) ≃ -ен-ие.
(5) ≃ -ник, -щик.

Examples: (1) Наро́дная арти́стка Украи́нской ССР (a title: 'People's Artiste of the Ukrainian SSR'). Cf. арти́ст, 'an artiste'.
(2) Вы́ставка маши́нных дета́лей (an exhibition of machine parts). Cf. вы́ставить, 'to show, present'.
(3) Перцо́вка — во́дка, насто́енная на пе́рце (pertsovka is a vodka with a pepper base). Cf. перцо́вый, 'pepper'.
(4) Зимо́вка в А́рктике (a winter stay in the Arctic). Cf. зимова́ть, 'to spend the winter'.
(5) Скре́пки продаю́тся в писчебума́жном магази́не (paperclips are sold at a stationer's). Cf. скрепи́ть, 'to secure, hold together'.
(6) Ре́дкая бе́лка на са́мом де́ле бела́ (very few squirrels are in fact white). Cf. бе́лый, 'white'.
(7) Он вы́скочка — ле́зет всю́ду (he's an upstart, expert at making his way). Cf. вы́скочить, 'to spring out'.

КОНТР- (КОНТРА-) [60+]

Prod: P.
App: Nouns and adjectives.
Lex: Opposition, 'counter-'.
Syn: ≃ анти-, противо-.
Ant: ≃ про-.
Example: Перешли́ в контрнаступле́ние (they went over to the counter-attack). Cf. наступле́ние, 'an attack'.

-ЛИВ- [150+]

Prod: P.
App: Infinitive stems of verbs. Stems of nouns.
Mut: к > ч, г > ж, х > ш, but -ск-, -зг-, are preserved.
Lex: Tending to show a certain quality.
Syn: = -чив-, ≃ -ист-.
Example: Шутли́вый разгово́р (a witty, amusing, conversation). Cf. шу́тка, 'a joke'.

-М- (-ЕМ-, -ОМ-) (250+]

Prod: P.
App: Present stems of transitive (and, rarely, of intransitive) verbs.
Lex: Potential, '-able, -ible'.
Syn: ≃ -тель-н-.
N.B.: This suffix is formally identical with that of the present passive participle, but unlike the latter may express non-actual, possible, qualities. With this

meaning it may be attached to the stems of perfective (as well as of imperfective) verbs. Adjectives in -м- are frequently prefixed by не- or compounded with an adverb, e.g. недопусти́мый (inadmissible), малоприменимый (rarely applicable).

Example: Челове́к с несгиба́емой во́лей (a man of inflexible will). Cf. сгиба́ть, 'to bend'.

МЕЖ- (МЕЖДУ-) [80+]

Prod: P.

App: Nouns of either foreign or native origin.

Lex: Position between objects, connecting objects, 'inter-'.

Syn: = интер-, ≃ внутри-.

Ant: ≃ вне-.

Example: Межплане́тное простра́нство (interplanetary space). Cf. плане́та, 'a planet'.

МИКРО- [70+]

Prod: P.

App: Nouns and adjectives.

Lex: Decrease in size or scope, 'micro-'.

Ant: = макро-.

Example: Микробиоло́гия — изуче́ние микро́бов (microbiology is the study of microbes). Cf. биоло́гия, 'biology'.

-Н[1]- [3900+/2500+]

Prod: (1) (2) VP. (3) P.

App: (1) (2) Stems of nouns and stems of adjectives (often of foreign origin). (3) Stems of verbs.

Str: (1) (2) (3) In all but thirty or so forms the stress remains as in the word of origin. These exceptions have stress on the termination (e.g. взрывно́й, 'explosive', from взрыв).

Lex: (1) Relating to *X* (where *X* is denoted by the word of origin).
(2) Possessing the qualities of *X*.
(3) Potential, '-able, -ible'.

Syn: (1) (2) ≃ -ск-.

N.B.: This suffix should not be confused with that originating in past passive participles in Old Russian (-н-, -ен-, -ён-), which is of participial meaning.

Examples: (1) Наро́дное образова́ние (popular education). Cf. наро́д, 'people'.
(2) Ре́альный дохо́д (real income). Cf. реали́ст, 'a realist'.
(3) Подвижна́я шкала́ (a sliding scale). Cf. подвига́ть, 'to move'.

НЕ- [300+/770+]

Prod: (1) P. (2) NP.

App: Nouns and adjectives.

Lex: (1) Negation, opposition, 'non-'. (2) Poor quality.

Syn: (1) ≃ без-. (2) ≃ о- (verbal).

Examples: (1) Я не допускáю невéжливости (I don't tolerate bad manners). Cf. вéжливый, 'polite'.

(2) Он проявля́л невнимáние к словáм собесéдника (he paid scant attention to what his companion was saying). Cf. внимáние, 'attention'.

НЕО- [50+]

Prod: P.

App: Nouns and adjectives of foreign origin.

Lex: Renewal, revival, 'neo-'.

Example: Алексéя Н. Толстóго мóжно считáть неореали́стом (A. N. Tolstoy may be called a neo-realist). Cf. реали́ст, 'a realist'.

-НИК [850+/360+]

Prod: (1) P. (2) (3) (4) (5) WP.

App: (1) Stems of nouns which may be deverbal and (uncommonly and now NP-ly) of verbal infinitives.

(2) (3) (4) Stems of nouns and of adjectives.

(5) Stems of nouns to which prefixes of 'spatial' meaning (на-, над-, о-, под-, пред-) are also added.

Mut: к > ч, г > ж, х > ш, ц > ч. (N.B. з remains unchanged.)

Soft: л only.

Lex: (1) Male persons by occupation, activity, adherence.

(2) Instruments.

(3) Containers.

(4) Collective nouns.

(5) Various: objects distinguished by a spatial relationship with objects denoted by the nouns of origin.

Syn: (1) ≃ -ец, -ёр, -ик, -щик.

(2) ≃ -к-а, -тель, -тор.

(3) ≃ -ниц-а.

Ant: (4) ≃ -ин-а.

N.B.: The suffix is occasionally found in new words with the interfix -ш-, as in эмгеýшник, 'a student at Moscow State University' (МГУ).

Examples: (1) Помóщник дирéктора (a deputy director). Cf. пóмощь (*f.*), 'help'.

(2) Температýра измеря́ется грáдусником (temperature is measured with a thermometer). Cf. грáдус, 'a degree'.

(3) Загналá кур в куря́тник (she chased the hens into the hen-house). Cf. кýры, 'hens'.

(4) Гóры покры́ты виногрáдниками (the hills are covered with vineyards). Cf. виногрáд, 'grapes'.

(5) Пропáвшая собáка нóсит ошéйник (the missing dog is wearing a collar). Cf. шéя, 'a neck'.

-НИЦ-А [350+/220+]

Prod: (1) P. (2) NP. (3) WP.

App: (1) Stems of nouns denoting male persons, stems of verbs.

(2) Stems of verbs.

(3) Stems of nouns (usually, masculine nouns).

Lex: (1) Female persons by occupation, activity, adherence.
(2) Places, instruments.
(3) Containers.
Syn: (1) = -щиц-а, ≃ -иц-а, -к-а.
(2) ≃ -иц-а.
(3) ≃ -ник.
Examples: (1) Тре́буется домрабо́тница (domestic worker wanted). Cf. рабо́тник, 'a worker' (*m.*).
(2) Спуска́ться по ле́стнице (to go downstairs). Cf. лезть, 'to climb'.
(3) Ребёнок опроки́нул пе́пельницу (the child upset the ashtray). Cf. пе́пел, 'ash'.

-НН- (-ЕНН-, -ЁНН-) [450+/10+]

Prod: P.
App: Infinitive stems of transitive verbs.
Str: As in the infinitive of the verb of origin, with rare exceptions.
Lex: Having undergone some action, '-ed'.
Example: Иллюстри́рованный журна́л (an illustrated magazine). Cf. иллюстра́ция, 'an illustration'.

-ОВ[2]- (-ЕВ-) [780+/270+]

Prod: (1) (2) VP.
App: Stems of nouns and (very rarely) of adjectives.
Str: No change if the noun of origin has fixed stress, as in берёзовый (birch-wood) from берёза (acc. берёзу, nom. pl. берёзы). Backward to the termination or (rarely) the suffix if the noun of origin has mobile stress, as in годово́й (annual) from год (gen. pl. годо́в).
Lex: (1) Made of an object, characteristic of an object.
(2) Characteristic of an object. (1) (2) Numerous indefinite relationships with the object denoted by the word of origin.
Syn: (1) (2) ≃ -н-, -ск-, -ь-.
Examples: (1) Кро́ликовая ша́пка (a cap made of rabbit skin). Cf. кро́лик, 'a rabbit'.
(2) Дождево́й червь (an earthworm). Cf. дождь, 'rain'.

-ОСТЬ (-ЕСТЬ) [100+/2360+]

Prod: VP.
App: Stems of adjectives, many of which are derived from verbs (and so already suffixed). These suffixes are normally retained.
Lex: Abstract ideas (an almost purely grammatical function).
Syn: ≃ -изн-а, -ин-а, -ств-о, -цин-а, -ье.
N.B.: -ость is frequently found as the second member of compound suffixes, the most common of which are -к-ость, -лив-ость, -м-ость, -н-ость, -нн-ость. The last three of these compound suffixes are very common, nouns with these suffixes making up 8, 48 and 16 per cent respectively of all forms ending in -ость, and appear to be regarded as units. The suffix -есть replaces -ость after stems in -ж and -ч, e.g. тя́жесть (weight), плову́честь (floatability).
Example: Он погрузи́лся в заду́мчивость (he became deep in thought). Cf. заду́мчивый, 'pensive'.

ПО- [100+]

Prod: (1) (2) P. (3) (4) WP.
App: Nouns, nearly all of native origin.
Lex: (1) Regularity of occurrence.
(2) Conformity to a standard.
(3) Position alongside an object.
(4) Posteriority.
Syn: (3) ≃ при-. (4) ≃ после-.
Ant: (4) = до-.
N.B. In adjectives often used with the suffix -н-.
Examples: (1) Почасова́я опла́та труда́ (pay by the hour). Cf. час, 'an hour'.
(2) Подохо́дный нало́г (income tax). Cf. дохо́д, 'income'.
(3) Пограни́чный отря́д (border patrol). Cf. грани́ца, 'a border'.
(4) Посме́ртные произведе́ния (posthumous works). Cf. смерть, 'death'.

ПОД- [200+/10+]

Prod: (1) (2) P. (3) WP.
App: Nouns, nearly all of native origin.
Lex: (1) Position below, beneath, an object, 'under-, hypo-'.
(2) Subordination, 'sub-, under'.
(3) Proximity.
Syn: (1) (2) = суб-. (3) ≃ при-.
Ant: (1) = над-. (2) ≃ над-.
N.B.: In adjectives always used with the suffix -н-.
Examples: (1) Подсне́жный лёд не та́ет (snow-covered ice does not melt). Cf. снег, 'snow'.
(2) В Сиби́ри живёт подви́д барсука́ — песча́ный (a sub-species of the badger, the sandy badger, lives in Siberia). Cf. вид, 'a species'.
(3) Пе́сня «Подмоско́вные Вечера́» ско́ро ста́ла о́чень популя́рной (the song 'Moscow Nights' soon became very popular). Cf. Москва́.

ПРЕД- [70+]

Prod: (1) (2) P.
App: Nouns, nearly all of native origin.
Lex: (1) Immediate anteriority, 'pre-'.
(2) Position in front of an object.
Syn: (1) ≃ до-.
Ant: (1) ≃ по-.
(2) ≃ за-.
N.B.: In adjectives always used with one of the suffixes -н-, -ск-.
Examples: (1) Предобе́денная прогу́лка (a walk before lunch). Cf. обе́д, 'lunch'.
(2) Преддве́рие театра́льного сезо́на (the threshold of the theatre season). Cf. дверь (*f.*), 'a door'.

ПРОТИВО- [60+]

Prod: P.
App: Nouns and adjectives.
Lex: Opposition, 'anti-, counter-'.
Syn: = анти-, ≃ контр-.
Ant: = про-.
Example: Противога́зовая ма́ска (a gas-mask). Cf. газ, 'gas'.

САМ-О- [300+]

Prod: P.
App: Nouns and adjectives, most of which are deverbal.
Lex: 'Self-, auto-'.
Syn: = авто-.
Example: Ме́стное самоуправле́ние (local self-government). Cf. управля́ть, 'to govern'.

СВЕРХ- [60+]

Prod: (1) P. (2) WP.
App: Nouns and adjectives.
Lex: (1) Superiority.
(2) Intensity.
Syn: (2) = пре-.
Ant: (1) ≃ суб-.
(2) ≃ -ов-ат-.
Examples: (1) Сверхсро́чная рабо́та (overtime). Cf. срок, 'a period'.
(2) Сверхмо́щный дви́гатель (a high-power motor). Cf. мо́щный, 'powerful'.

-СК- (-ЕСК-, -ЦК-) [750+/1730+]

Prod: VP.
App: Stems of masculine (and, rarely, feminine) nouns.
Mut: к > ч, г > ж, х > ш before -ск-, in most cases. к > ч, г > ж, х > ш, ц > ч, з > ж before -еск-. Where a noun with the stem consonant к denotes a person, combination with the ending -ск- often produces the group -цк-, as in дура́цкий (fool's). This group is also found in inanimate nouns but is here rare. Many words of recent formation do not exhibit these mutations, e.g. Узбе́кская ССР (the Uzbek SSR).
Soft: л only.
Str: No change in nearly all cases. Exceptionally the stress moves on to the termination, as in городско́й (urban).
Lex: Belonging to or characteristic of some person or place.
Syn: ≃ -н-.
N.B.: The adjective suffixes -ск-, -н-, are of very general meaning and may often be used with the same stem. In these cases a difference in emphasis in the meanings of -ск- and -н- may be clearly seen. The former suffix classifies, the latter usually denotes quality. Compare траги́ческий стиль and траги́чная у́часть (fate). It should be remembered, however, that the

meanings of the two suffixes coincide to a very great extent. The suffixes -ие, -ия, of nouns such as житие́ (life story), а́рмия (army), are replaced by the syllable -ей- when the suffix -ск- is added (to give, for example, жите́йский, арме́йский). The suffix -ск- is used with many derived (already affixed) stems. In some cases the identity of the first affix is preserved and may be assigned a meaning (as in -ист-ск-, -ич-еск-) but for the most part the first and second affixes combine functionally to express a meaning identical with that of -ск- (this is true of -ен-ск-, -иан-ск-, -ий-ск-, -ч-еск-).

Example: Иссле́довательская рабо́та (research work). Cf. иссле́довать, 'to investigate'.

-СТВ-О (-ЕСТВ-) [550+/360+]

Prod: (1) (2) P. (3) NP.

App: (1) Stems of nouns, adjectives.

(2) Nouns denoting male persons, stems of verbs.

(3) Stems of verbs.

Mut: к > ч, г > ж, х > ш before the alternative form -еств-о.

Lex: (1) Qualities, occupations, spheres of activity.

(2) Groups of people.

(3) Actions or results of action.

Syn: ≃ -ч-еств-о, -ье.

N.B.: The form -еств-о is found after the stem-consonants ж, ч, ш, щ, only.

Examples: (1) Э́то сде́лано не про́сто, а с лука́вством (there's more to this than meets the eye). Cf. лука́вый, 'cunning'.

(2) Сове́тское прави́тельсво (the Soviet government). Cf. пра́вить, 'to govern'.

(3) Ору́дия произво́дства (the means of production). Cf. производи́ть, 'to produce'.

-ТЕЛЬ [450+]

Prod: (1) VP. (2) P.

App: (1) (2) Infinitive stems of verbs, nearly all of which are transitive.

Str: In nouns derived from verbs in -еть, -ить, the stress is always penultimate, as in граби́тель (a robber) from гра́бить. No change in other nouns, e.g. вая́тель (a sculptor), се́ятель (a sower).

Lex: (1) Male persons distinguished by actions, '-er'.

(2) Instruments, '-er'.

Syn: (1) ≃ -ик, -ник, -ор, -щик.

(2) ≃ -ник, -ор.

N.B.: A formally and functionally similar suffix -итель, as in ревни́тель (a zealot), is now unproductive. Female equivalents of nouns in -тель (1) are formed by the addition of a second suffix, -ниц-а.

Examples: (1) Го́сти бесе́довали с руководи́телями КПСС (the visitors talked with CPSU leaders). Cf. руководи́ть, 'to guide'.

(2) Показа́тели проду́кции (indicators of production, production figures). Cf. показа́ть, 'to show'.

-ЧИВ- [70+]

Prod: VP.

App: Stems of verbs (or of deverbal nouns) which are prefixed in nearly all cases.

Lex: Tendency to exhibit a certain quality, '-ish'.

Syn: = -лив-.

Example: Нахóдчивый отвéт (a resourceful reply). Cf. находи́ть, 'to find'.

-Ш-А [60+/30+]

Prod: (1) P. (2) NP.

App: Stems of masculine nouns denoting occupation or profession.

Soft: л only.

Lex: (1) Female equivalents to the male persons denoted by the nouns to the stems of which the suffix is added.
(2) Wives of the persons denoted by the nouns of origin (rare).

Syn: (1) (2) ≃ -их-а. (1) ≃ -иц-а, -ниц-а, -щиц-а.

N.B.: Unlike the stems of nouns in -их-а the stems used with -ш-а are nearly all of foreign origin.

Examples: (1) Библиотéкарша завéдует кни́гами (the librarian is in charge of the books). Cf. библиотéкарь, 'librarian' (*m.*).
(2) Миллионéрша.

-Щ- (-АЩ-, -УЩ-, -ЮЩ-, -ЯЩ-) [180+]

Prod: P.

App: Stems of intransitive (rarely, transitive) verbs.

Lex: Characteristics (usually permanent).

Syn: ≃ -н-, -тель-н-.

N.B.: The vowel preceding the consonant щ may be considered as part of the affix. It varies (*a*) according to the conjugation of the verb from which the adjective is to be derived (у, ю *versus* а, я) and (*b*) according to the hardness or softness of the final stem-consonant (у, а *versus* ю, я). Adjectives formed with this affix are participial in origin and some may occasionally be used as participles.

Example: Э́то настоя́щий прáздник (this is a real holiday). Cf. стоя́ть, 'to stand'.

-ЩИК (-ЧИК) [670+/280+]

Prod: (1) (2) P.

App: (1) Stems of nouns and verbs (of either aspect).
(2) Stems of transitive verbs.

Soft: л only.

Str: (1) Fixed in all but a very few cases, e.g. покупщи́к.
(2) No change.

Lex: (1) Male persons by occupation or activity, or by objects connected with their occupation.
(2) Instruments.

Syn: (1) ≃ -ёр, -ик, -ник, -тель.
(2) ≃ -к-а, -ник, -тель.

Examples: (1) Болéльщики футбóла (football fans). Cf. болéть, 'to support enthusiastically'.

(2) Автомати́ческий загру́зчик (an automatic loader). Cf. загрузи́ть, 'to load'.

-ЩИН-А (-ЧИН-, -ЛЬ-ЩИН-) [100+/15+]

Prod: (1) P. (2) WP.

App: (1) Stems of adjectives with suffixes -н-, -ск-, e.g. ба́рский (lord's), stems of nouns.

(2) Stems of place names (chiefly in West Russia).

Lex: (1) Ideas and institutions which are disapproved of.

(2) Names of districts.

Syn: (1) ≃ -ость.

Examples: (1) Устрани́ть казёнщину в литерату́ре (get rid of conventionalism in literature). Cf. казённый, 'official'.

(2) Брига́да из Ха́рьковщины оккупи́ровала го́род (a brigade from the Khar'kov district occupied the town). Cf. Ха́рьков.

-ЩИЦ-А (-ЧИЦ-) [170+/80+]

Prod: P.

App: Stems of masculine nouns in -щик/-чик, -ль-щик, stems of verbs.

Lex: Female persons by occupation, activity.

Syn: = -ниц-а, ≃ -к-а, -ш-а.

Example: Она́ ста́ла автома́тчицей (she became a machine-minder). Cf. автома́т, 'an automatic machine'.

-Ь- (see below) [30+/20+]

Prod: (1) (2) P.

App: (1) Stems of nouns denoting persons (usually with a suffix ending in -к, -иц-а, e.g. мужи́к, деви́ца).

(1) (2) Stems of nouns denoting animals.

Mut: к > ч, г > ж, х > ш; ц > ч; т > ч, д > ж.

Soft: All.

Lex: (1) Appurtenance, ''s'.

(2) Being made from some part of an animal.

N.B.: This suffix (jod) is not written separately from the adjective terminations, which appear as -ий, -ья, -ье; -ьи in the nominative.

Examples: (1) деви́чья фами́лия (a maiden name). Cf. деви́ца, 'a maiden'.

(2) медве́жья ша́пка (a bearskin cap). Cf. медве́дь (*m.*), 'a bear'.

-ЬЕ (-ИЕ) [200+/2920+]

Prod: (1) (2) P.

App: (1) Stems of nouns.

(2) Stems of adjectives, a few noun stems with prefixes, and a few multiple stems (adjective and noun) with which the suffix forms compound words, e.g. вольноду́м-ие.

Mut: к > ч, г > ж, х > ш.

Soft: All.

Lex: (1) Places, positions.

(2) Qualities.

Syn: (2) ≃ -ин-а, -ость, -ств-о, -щин-а.

N.B.: The suffix with meaning (1) is only found in nouns with a prefix of 'spatial' meaning (вз-, за-, по-, etc.). The noun Заполя́рье (the Polar region) is formed exceptionally from an adjective stem.

Examples: (1) Прово́дим ле́то на взмо́рье (we spend the summer at the coast). Cf. мо́ре, 'sea'.

(2) На разду́мье дано́ три́дцать секу́нд (you are given thirty seconds to think). Cf. ду́мы, 'thoughts'.

9

A LIST OF AFFIXES

The following list contains all affixes registered in at least five words in present-day Russian. Further details of the functions of the commonest prefixes and suffixes are given in §8.

The information presented in each section of the list is arranged as follows. The section is headed by a simple affix. Underneath is a numeral or pair of numerals in square brackets indicating the number of recorded words in which the affix is found.

A single numeral is used for an affix always found alone, a double numeral for an affix which can be part of a compound prefix or suffix. Thus the figures [350+/60+] placed below the suffix -ИН-А indicate that this affix is found in over 410 words, in over 350 of which it stands alone (as in бара́н-ин-а, 'mutton') and in over 60 of which it is preceded by another suffix or suffixes (as in сердц-ев-и́н-а, 'the stone of a fruit'). The sign + that follows all of these numerals is intended as a reminder both that figures are rounded to the nearest ten below (five below if under twenty) and that the lists of words on which the figures are based are possibly incomplete.[1]

One of the abbreviations VP, P, WP, NP, placed in round brackets below the numerals, shows the highest degree of productiveness exhibited by the affix.

Where an affix is productive in varying degrees according to application or function, an abbreviation is placed after each example illustrating each of the applications or functions in which productiveness is limited. The suffix -ИН-А, for instance, is productive (P) as an expression of singulative meaning, as in соло́м-

[1] Sources of the figures: Bielfeldt (1958), Ozhegov and Shapiro (1957), Ushakov (1935–40).

ин-а (a straw), but is only weakly productive (WP) in words denoting kinds of meat, e.g. бара́н-ин-а. Isolatable but probably unperceived affixes are marked (*Isol. only*). The examples illustrating the use of each affix consist of a pair of words (the first without, the second with, the affix), each of which is followed by an English translation or explanation. The lexical meanings of each affix are distinguished as far as possible, and each of these meanings (marked with a Roman numeral) is illustrated by at least one example. An attempt has been made in providing several examples for each lexical function to show all the kinds of stem to which the affix is commonly added.

Beneath the entry for the simple affix are listed the compound affixes into which it enters as either the first item (if a prefix) or the last (if a suffix). These compound affixes are listed in order of frequency of occurrence.

Superscript numerals (as in -ИН^{2}-) are used to distinguish affixes of the same form but of widely different functions. In addition a superscript zero (as in пре-по^{0}-) is used in compound affixes to denote a lexically meaningless element.

The abbreviations *Arch.*, *Poet.*, *Pop.*, following some examples denote that the word quoted is archaic, poetic or most common in uneducated speech. An asterisk indicates that the addition of an affix causes mutation (see §4E and §8).

The list does *not* include:

(*a*) Affixes occurring in less than five words, such as the compound -Щ-АВ- as in сухоща́вый (lean).

(*b*) Elements that are by origin affixes but which are not perceived or isolatable as such. These elements may be either Slavonic (as in бул-ава́, 'a mace', вес-ть, 'news') or non-Slavonic (as in гра́д-ус, 'a degree', аб-дика́ция, 'abdication').

(*c*) The endings -а, -я; -о, -е denoting gender only. These endings are written separately within suffixes to facilitate comparisons (e.g. between Б-А and -Б-ИЩ-Е) but they should not be regarded as affixes in the sense in which the term is used in this work.

А- [20+] (WP)	I норма́льный, 'normal'; анорма́льный, 'abnormal, non-normal'
-АВ-	See -ЯВ-
АВТО- [200+] (P)	I портре́т, 'portrait'; автопортре́т, 'self-portrait'

-АГО [?] (NP)	живóй, 'living, lively'; Живáго (the surname Zhivago)
-АДА (*Isol. only*) [20+]	колóнна, 'a column'; колоннáда, 'a colonnade'
-АЖ [70+] (P)	I километр, 'kilometre'; километрáж, 'distance in kilometres' II картóн, 'cardboard'; картонáж, 'articles made of cardboard' (NP)
-АЙ (-ЯЙ, -ЕЙ) [10+/5+] (NP)	I обы́чный, 'usual'; обы́чай, 'a custom' II богáтый, 'rich'; богатéй (*Pop.*), 'a rich man'
-ат^0-ай [5+]	глядéть, 'to look'; соглядáтай, 'a spy' всегдá, 'always'; завсегдáтай, 'an habitué'
-АК (-ЯК) [150+/50+] (WP)	I Áвстрия, 'Austria'; австрия́к, 'an Austrian' II ры́ба, 'a fish'; рыбáк, 'a fisherman' (NP) III дóбрый, 'kind, good'; добря́к, 'a kind-hearted person' (NP)
-н-як [30+]	I дуб, 'an oak tree'; дубня́к, 'a group of oak trees' II горá, 'a hill'; гóрный, 'mining'; горня́к, 'a miner'
-л-як [10+]	свет, 'light'; свéтлый, 'light'; светля́к, 'a glow-worm, fire-fly' мёрзнуть, 'to freeze'; мёрзлый, 'frozen'; мерзля́к, 'someone who feels the cold'
-ч^0-ак (-чак?) [10+]	I смéлый, 'daring'; смельчáк, 'a bold man' II соль (*f.*), 'salt'; солёный, солóный, 'salty'; солончáк, 'a salt marsh'
-АК-А [10+] (NP)	I зевáть, 'to yawn'; зевáка, 'an idler'
-АН [20+] (NP)	I поли́тика, 'politics'; политикáн, 'a self-seeking politician' I грýбый, 'coarse'; грубия́н, 'a lout, bully'
-АНТ (-ЯНТ) [100+] (P)	I кýрсы, 'courses of study'; курсáнт, 'a student' I эмигри́ровать, 'to emigrate'; эмигрáнт, 'an émigré'
АНТИ- [120+] (P)	I общéственный, 'social'; антиобщéственный, 'anti-social'

*-АР (-ЯР) [15+] (NP)	I овца́, 'a sheep'; овча́р, 'a shepherd' I стол, 'a table'; столя́р, 'a joiner'
АРХИ- [10+] (P)	I глу́пый, 'stupid'; архиглу́пый, 'very stupid indeed' I скéптик, 'a sceptic'; архискéптик, 'a confirmed sceptic'
-АРЬ [70+] (WP)	I звон, 'a ringing noise, peal of bells'; звона́рь (*m.*), 'a bell-ringer' II сухо́й, 'dry'; суха́рь (*m.*), 'a rusk' (NP)
-АСТ- (-ЯСТ-) [40+] (WP)	I глаз, 'an eye'; глаза́стый, 'with big eyes' I у́хо, 'an ear'; у́ши, 'ears'; уша́стый, 'with big ears'
*-АТ^{1}- [50+/200+] (WP)	I клеёнка, 'oilcloth, -skin'; клеёнчатый (костюм), 'oilskin(s)' II во́лосы, 'hair'; волоса́тый, 'hairy' (NP)
-ов-ат^{1}- (-ев-) [100+]	I го́рький, 'bitter'; горькова́тый, 'rather bitter' (-ов^{2}-) II у́гол, 'a corner'; углова́тый, 'angular, awkward' (-ов^{0}-)
-ч^{0}-ат^{1}- [100+]	зуб, 'a tooth, cog'; зубча́тый, 'toothed, cogged'
-АТ^{2} (*Isol. only*) [70+]	I делега́ция, 'a delegation'; делега́т, 'a delegate' II рефери́ровать, 'to summarize'; рефера́т, 'a summary' III дирéктор, 'a director'; директора́т, 'a directorate' IV фо́сфор, 'phosphorus'; фосфа́т, 'phosphate'
-АЧ [50+] (WP)	I борода́, 'a beard'; борода́ч, 'a bearded man' II ло́вкий, 'nimble'; ловка́ч, 'an agile man' (NP)
-АШ	See -ЯШ
-Б-А [30+] (NP)	I пали́ть, 'to fire, shoot'; пальба́, 'firing' II суди́ть, 'to judge, decide'; судьба́, 'fate'
БЕЗ- (БЕЗЪ-, БЕС-) [450+/25+] (VP)	I врéдный, 'harmful'; безврéдный, 'harmless' II воло́с, 'hair', *gen. pl.*; безволо́сый, 'hairless' (WP)
без-от- [20+]	отлага́ть, 'to postpone'; безотлага́тельный, 'urgent'

без-вы- [5+]	вы́ход, 'an exit'; безвы́ходное положе́ние, 'a hopeless position'
В- (ВО-) (*verbal*) [500+]	класть, 'to lay'; вкла́дывать, 'to put in, invest'; вклад, 'a deposit, investment, contribution'
-В-А [10+] (NP)	I моли́ться, 'to pray'; моли́тва, 'praying, a prayer'
ВЗ- (ВЗО-, ВС-) (*verbal*) [350+]	лете́ть, 'to fly'; взлете́ть, 'to fly upwards'; взлёт, 'upward flight, take-off'
ВИЦЕ- [10+] (NP)	I адмира́л, 'an admiral'; вице-адмира́л, 'vice-admiral'
ВНЕ- [40+] (P)	I брак, 'marriage'; внебра́чный, 'illegitimate' I план, 'a plan'; внепла́новый, 'not covered by the plan'
ВНУТРИ- [40+] (P)	I па́ртия, 'a party, group'; внутрипарти́йный, 'inner-party, within the party' I вид, 'a species'; внутривидово́й, 'intraspecific'
-В-О (*-ИВ-, -ЕВ-) [10+] (NP)	I пить, 'to drink'; пи́во, 'beer' I топи́ть, 'to heat'; то́пливо, 'fuel'
ВОЗ- (ВОС-) (*verbal*) [200+/15+]	рожда́ть, 'to bear, give birth'; возрожда́ть, 'to revive, regenerate'; возрожде́ние, 'revival, Renascence'
вос-при- [10+]	приня́ть, 'to accept'; восприня́ть, 'to perceive'; восприя́тие, 'perception'
вос-про-из- [5+]	произвести́, 'to produce'; воспроизвести́, 'to reproduce'; воспроизведе́ние, 'reproduction, a reproduction'
ВСЕ- [20+] (NP)	I сла́вный, 'glorious'; всесла́вный, 'all-glorious, most glorious'
ВЫ- (*verbal*) [800+]	ходи́ть, 'to walk'; выходи́ть, 'to walk out'; вы́ход, 'an exit'
-ДА [5+] (NP)	I пра́вый, 'right, true'; пра́вда, 'truth'

ДЕ- (*before consonant*) — I мобилиза́ция, 'mobilization'; демобилиза́ция, 'demobilization'

(ДЕЗ-) (*before vowel*) — I инфе́кция, 'contagion'; дезинфе́кция, 'disinfection'

For exceptions to the above rule see §8

[200+]
(P)

ДИС-
(ДИЗ-)
[15+]
(WP) — I гармо́ния, 'harmony'; дисгармо́ния, 'discordance'

ДО-
(*verbal*)
[500+] — по́лный, 'full'; допо́лнить, 'to add, supplement'; дополне́ние, 'a supplement'

ДО-
[10+]
(P) — I война́, 'war, a war'; довое́нный, 'pre-war'
I Пётр, 'Peter'; допетро́вский, 'pre-Petrine'

-ЕВ — See -ОВ[1,2]

-ЕВ-О — See -В-О

-ЕЙ — See -АЙ

-ЕК — See -ОК

-ЕЛЬ
[15+]
(NP) — I ги́бнуть, 'to perish'; ги́бель (*f.*), 'ruin'
II кача́ть, 'to swing, rock'; каче́ли (*pl.*), 'a swing'
See also -ТЕЛЬ

-ЕЛЬ — (As in чита́тель, 'a reader'; учи́тель, 'a teacher')
See -ТЕЛЬ

-ЕМ- — See -М-

-ЕН- — See -Н[2]-

-ЕН-ИЕ — See -ЬЕ

-ЕНН-
(-ЯНН-)
[70+/150+]
(P) — I число́, 'a number'; безчи́сленный, 'innumerable'
II здоро́вый, 'healthy'; здорове́нный (*Pop.*), 'very healthy' (NP)
See also -НН-

-ств-енн-
(-еств-)
[120+] — сре́дний, 'middle'; посре́дственный, 'mediocre'
госуда́рство, 'a state'; госуда́рственный, 'state'

-в-енн-
[15+] — бри́ться, 'to shave, get shaved'; бри́тва, 'a razor, a shave'; бри́твенный прибо́р, 'a shaving kit'

-зн-енн-
[10+] — боле́ть, 'to be ill'; боле́знь (*f.*), 'an illness'; боле́зненный, 'ailing, morbid'

-н^0-ов^0-енн- [5+]		обы́чай, 'a custom'; обыкнове́нный, 'usual' проники́нуть, 'to penetrate'; проникнове́нный го́лос, 'a voice filled with emotion'
-тель-ств-енн- [5+]		обстоя́тельство, 'a circumstance'; обстоя́тельственный, 'circumstantial'
-ЕНТ [15+] (WP)	I	рецензи́ровать, 'to review (a book)'; рецензе́нт, 'a reviewer'
-ЕР (*Isol. only*) [10+/20+]	I	фе́рма, 'a farm'; фе́рмер, 'a farmer'
	II	танк, 'a tank'; та́нкер, 'an oil tanker'
-ион-ер [20+]		револю́ция, 'a revolution'; революционе́р, 'a revolutionary'
-ЕСК-		See -СК-
-ЕСС-А [5+] (NP)	I	принц, 'a prince'; принце́сса, 'a princess'
-ЕСТВ-О		See -СТВ-О
-ЕЦ [600+/230+] (VP)	I	го́ры, 'mountains'; го́рец, 'a mountain dweller'
	II	комсомо́л, 'Young Communist organization'; комсомо́лец, 'Young Communist'
	II	просвеще́ние, 'education'; просвеще́нец, 'a worker in education'
	III	отве́ргнуть, 'to reject'; отве́рженный, 'rejected'; отве́рженец, 'an outcast' (NP)
	IV	жить, 'to live'; жиле́ц, 'an inhabitant, occupier' (NP)
	V	ре́зать, 'to cut'; резе́ц, 'a cutting tool' (NP)
		Plus other functions which are difficult to define
-ан^0-ец [50+]		А́фрика, 'Africa'; африка́нец, 'an African'
-ен^0-ец [50+]		молодо́й, 'young'; младе́нец, 'an infant'
-л^0-ец [40+]		страда́ть, 'to suffer'; страда́лец, 'a martyr'
-ов^0-ец [30+]		кружо́к, 'a club'; кружко́вец, 'a member of a club'
-ин^1-ец [20+]		Ба́ку (the town of Baku); ба́кинец, 'a native of Baku'
-иан^0-ец (-ьян-) [10+]		Ма́льтус (the economist Malthus); мальтузиа́нец, 'a Malthusian'
		вегета́ция, 'vegetation'; вегетариа́нец, 'a vegetarian'
-л^0-ен^0-ец [10+]		приспосо́бить, 'to adapt'; приспособле́нец, 'a time-server, opportunist'

-н-ец [10+]		брать, 'to take'; новобра́нец, 'a recruit'
-ав^{0}-ец [5+]		краси́вый, 'handsome'; краса́вец, 'a handsome man'
-ин^{2}-ец [5+]		зверь (*m.*), 'a wild animal'; звери́нец, 'a menagerie'
-ЁЖ [20+] (WP)	I	гра́бить, 'to steal'; грабёж, 'theft'
-ЁН-		See -Н^{2}-
-ЁН-А [5+] (NP)	I	гуля́ть, 'to walk, have a good time'; гулёна (*Pop.*), 'a person fond of enjoyment'
*-ЁР [30+] (P)	I I	гримирова́ть, 'to apply make-up'; гримёр, 'a make-up man' шум, 'a noise'; шумёр, 'a sound-effects man'
-ЁХ-А		See -ОХ-А
ЗА- (*verbal*) [1400+/5+]		крыть, 'to cover'; закры́ть, 'to close'; закрытие, 'the act of closing' купи́ть, 'to buy'; закупи́ть, 'to lay in a stock'; заку́пка, 'purchasing, a purchase'
ЗА- [15+/5+] (P)	I I I	го́род, 'a town'; за́городный, 'out-of-town' рубе́ж, 'a boundary'; зарубе́жный, 'foreign' Кавка́з, 'Caucasus'; закавка́зский, 'Trans-Caucasian'
за^{0}-у- [5+]		уны́ть, 'to be dejected'; зауны́вный, 'mournful' ряд, 'a row, line'; заря́дный, 'commonplace'
-ЗНЬ [5+] (NP)	I	жить, 'to live'; жизнь (*f.*), 'life'
-ИВ- [50+] (NP)	I II	лень (*f.*), 'indolence, laziness'; лени́вый, 'lazy' вошь (*f.*), 'a louse'; вши́вый, 'louse-infected' See also -ЛИВ-, -ЧИВ-
-ИЕ		See -ЬЕ
ИЗ- (ИЗО-, ИЗЪ-, ИС-) (*verbal*) [300+]		че́рпать, 'to scoop, ladle'; исче́рпать, 'to exhaust'; исче́рпанность, 'exhaustion, comprehensive treatment' положи́ть, 'to lay down'; изложи́ть, 'to expound'; изложе́ние, 'an exposition'
-ИЗМ [300+/130+] (P)	I	тури́ст, 'a tourist'; тури́зм, 'tourism, holiday-making'

	I	большеви́к, 'a bolshevik'; большеви́зм, 'bolshevism'
-ал-изм [50+]		импе́рия, 'an empire'; империали́зм, 'imperialism'
-ат^{0}-изм [20+]		до́гма, 'a dogma'; догмати́зм, 'dogmatism'
-ан^{0}-изм [15+]		Аме́рика, 'America'; американи́зм, 'Americanism, an Americanism'
-ар-изм [10+]		парла́мент, 'parliament'; парламентари́зм, 'parliamentarism'
-ин-изм [10+]		А́льпы, 'the Alps'; альпини́зм, 'mountaineering'
-ион-изм [10+]		реви́зия, 'a revision'; ревизиони́зм, 'revisionism'
-иц-изм [10+]		кри́тик, 'a critic'; критици́зм, 'criticism'
-ив-изм [5+]		субъе́кт, 'a subject'; субъективи́зм, 'subjectivism'
-ИЗН-А [15+] (NP)	I	бе́лый, 'white'; белизна́, 'whiteness'
-ИЙ, -J-, -jod-		See -Ь^{1}-
-ИК† [300+/120+] (P)	I	вече́рний, 'evening'; вече́рник, 'evening course student'
	I	зубно́й, 'dental'; зубни́к, 'dentist'
	I	хи́мия, 'chemistry'; хи́мик, 'a chemist'
	II	безбо́жный, 'atheistic'; безбо́жник, 'an atheist'
	II	спле́тня, 'gossip'; спле́тник, 'a gossip, scandalmonger' (NP)
	III	ста́вить, 'to place, stand'; ста́вленный, 'placed'; ста́вленник, 'a protégé' (WP)
	IV	тупо́й, 'blunt, dull'; тупи́к, 'a blind alley' (WP)
	IV	у́тренний, 'morning'; у́тренник, 'a matinée, morning frost' (WP)
	IV	грузово́й, 'cargo'; грузови́к, 'a lorry' (WP)
-ов^{2}-ик (-ев-) [80+]		бро́ня́, 'armour'; броневи́к, 'an armoured car'
-ат^{2}-ик [15+]		до́гма, 'dogma'; догма́тик, 'a dogmatist'
-ян-ик [10+]		жесть (*f.*), 'tin'; жестя́ник, 'a tinsmith'

† Many forms in -ик may be analysed in two ways, e.g.: вече́р-н-ик/вече́р-ник. These are listed and counted once only, under -ик or -ник.

-ат^1-ик [5+]		во́лос, 'a hair'; волоса́тик, 'a kind of worm, a kind of crystal', etc.
-ен-ик [5+]		учи́ть, 'to teach, learn'; учени́к, 'a pupil'
-ер-ик [5+]		пять, пя́теро, 'five'; пятери́к, 'five units, e.g. horses'
-ИКА (*Isol. only*) [170+/30+]		динами́зм, 'dynamism'; дина́мика, 'dynamics'
-ист-ика [30+]		фолькло́р, 'folklore'; фольклори́стика, 'the study of folklore'
-ИН^1 (-ЫН) [250+/50+] (P)	I	до́чка, 'daughter'; до́чкин, 'daughter's'
	I	дя́дя, 'uncle'; дя́дин, 'uncle's'
	I	бе́лка, 'a squirrel'; бе́лкин, 'belonging to a squirrel' (WP)
	II	бе́лка, 'a squirrel'; Бе́лкин (fem. Бе́лкина, the surname Belkin) (NP)
	III	Гру́зия, 'Georgia'; грузи́н, 'a Georgian'
*-ан-ин^1 [40+]		го́род, 'a town'; горожа́нин, 'a town dweller'
-ч-ан-ин^1 [5+]		А́нглия, 'England'; англича́нин, 'an Englishman'
-ИН^2- [30+] (WP)	I	мышь (*f.*), 'a mouse'; мыши́ный, 'mouse, mouse-'
	I	ку́ры, 'hens'; кури́ный, 'hen-, hen-like'
-ИН^3 [30+/5+] (WP)	I	са́хар, 'sugar'; сахари́н, 'saccharine'
-ат-ин^3 [5+]		па́нкреас, 'the pancreas'; панкреати́н, 'pancreatin'
-ИН-А [350+/60+] (P)	I	соло́ма, 'straw'; соло́мина, 'a straw'
	II	бара́н, 'a ram'; бара́нина, 'mutton' (WP)
	II	теля́та, 'calves'; теля́тина, 'veal' (NP)
	III	морщи́ть, 'to wrinkle'; морщи́на, 'a wrinkle, crease' (WP)
	III	ква́сить, 'to pickle'; ква́шеный, 'pickled'; квашени́на, 'pickled cabbage' (WP)
	IV	вели́кий, 'large, great'; величина́, 'size' (NP)
-ов^2-ин-а (-ев-) [35+]		се́рдце, 'a heart'; сердцеви́на, 'the stone of a fruit'
		ди́кий, 'wild'; дико́вина, 'something wonderful'
-ят^0-ин-а [30+]		козёл, 'a goat'; козля́тина, 'goat-meat'
-ИН-О [?] (WP)	I	пу́шка, 'a cannon'; Пу́шкин (the surname Pushkin); Пу́шкино (the village of Pushkino)

	I	кольчу́га, ‘chain-mail’; Кольчу́гино (the village of Kol’chugino)
ИНТЕР- [30+] (WP)	I	вока́льный, ‘vocalic’; интервока́льный, ‘inter-vocalic’
-ИН-Я		See -ЫН-Я
-ИС-А [5+] (NP)	I	актёр, ‘an actor’; актри́са, ‘an actress’
-ИСТ^{1} [300+/80+] (P)	I	связь (*f.*), ‘connection, communication(s)’; связи́ст, ‘a signaller’
	I	социали́зм, ‘socialism’; социали́ст, ‘a socialist’
-ал-ист^{1} [40+]		мате́рия, ‘matter’; материали́ст, ‘a materialist’
-ион-ист^{1} [15+]		коллабора́ция, ‘collaboration’; коллаборациони́ст, ‘a collaborator’
-ив-ист^{1} [5+]		субъе́кт, ‘a subject’; субъективи́ст, ‘a subjectivist’
-ИСТ^{2}- [240+/10+] (VP)	I	волна́, ‘a wave’; волни́стый, ‘wavy, corrugated’
	II	напо́р, ‘pressure’; напо́ристый, ‘energetic’ (P)
-ян-ист^{2}- [10+]		ма́сло, ‘butter’; масляни́стый, ‘buttery, resembling butter’
-ИТ^{1} [40+] (WP)	I	бро́нхи, ‘bronchial tubes’; бронхи́т, ‘bronchitis’
-ИТ^{2} [40+] (WP)	I	динами́ческий, ‘dynamic’; динами́т, ‘dynamite’
	I	камы́ш, ‘cane, reeds’; камыши́т (a building material made of pressed cane and clay)
	I	малахи́т, ‘malachite’
-ИТ^{3} [5+] (NP)	I	митропо́лия, ‘an ecclesiastical province’; митрополи́т, ‘a Metropolitan’
-ИТ^{4}- [15+/15+] (NP)	I	знаменова́ть, ‘to signify’; знамени́тый, ‘celebrated, famous’
-ов^{2}-ит^{4}- [15+]		дар, ‘a gift’; дарови́тый, ‘gifted’
-ИТЕЛЬ [5+] (NP)	I	спасти́, ‘to save’; спаси́тель, ‘rescuer’
	I	ревнова́ть, ‘to be jealous’; ревни́тель, ‘a zealous follower, supporter’
		See also -ТЕЛЬ

*-ИХ-А	I	трус, 'a coward'; труси́ха, 'a cowardly woman'
[30+/10+]	I	портно́й, 'a tailor'; портни́ха, 'a dressmaker'
(P)	II	кро́лик, 'a rabbit'; крольчи́ха, 'a doe rabbit'
	III	по́вар, 'a chef'; повари́ха, 'a chef's wife' (WP)
-нич-их-а [5+]		дво́рничиха, 'wife of a дво́рник'
-ч-их-а [5+]		плове́ц, 'a swimmer' (*m.*); пловчи́ха, 'a swimmer' (*f.*)
-ИЦ-А†	I	лени́вец, 'a lazy man'; лени́вица, 'a lazy woman'
[120+/5+]	I	царь (*m.*), 'an emperor'; цари́ца, 'an empress' (NP)
(WP)	II	(*Pop.*) неле́пый, 'senseless, foolish'; неле́пица, 'a foolish saying or action'
	II	путь (*m.*), 'a road, way'; распу́тица, 'the season when the roads are bad'
	II	рабо́та, 'work'; безрабо́тица, 'unemployment'
	III	лев, 'a lion'; льви́ца, 'a lioness' (NP)
	IV	больно́й, 'painful, ill'; больни́ца, 'a hospital' (NP)
	V	пьяный, 'drunk'; пья́ница, 'a drunkard'
-лив-иц-а [5+]		сон, 'sleep'; сонли́вица, 'a sleepy woman'
-ИЧ	I	Лука́, 'Luke'; Луки́ч, 'the son of Luke'
[10+/?]	II	Псков (the town of Pskov); пско́вич, 'an inhabitant of Pskov'
(WP)	II	Омск (the town of Omsk); о́мич, 'an inhabitant of Omsk'
-ов^1-ич (-ев-)		царь (*m.*), 'a tsar'; царе́вич, 'the son of a tsar, a Crown Prince'
[?]		Григо́рий (the Christian name Gregory); Григо́ревич (the surname Grigorevich)
-ИЩ-Е [50+/40+] (NP)	I	го́род, 'a town'; городи́ще, 'the site of an ancient town'
-л^0-ищ-е [20+]		храни́ть, 'to store, keep'; храни́лище, 'a store, safe place'
-ов^2-ищ-е	I	стан, 'a camp'; станови́ще, 'a camp site'
[15+]	II	чу́до, 'a wonder'; чудо́вище, 'a monster'
-б-ищ-е [10+]		пасти́, 'to graze cattle'; па́стбище, 'a pasture, place for grazing'
-ИЯ		эмо́ция, 'an emotion' (cf. Fr. *émotion*)
(*Isol. only*)		симпа́тия, 'sympathy' (cf. Fr. *sympathie*)
[900+/400+]		спектро́метр, 'a spectrometer'; спектроме́трия, 'spectrometry'

† The remarks applying to -ИК/-НИК hold good also for -ИЦ-А/-НИЦ-А.

-ац-ия [200+]		рекомендова́ть, 'to recommend'; рекоменда́ция, 'a recommendation'
-из-ац-ия [120+]		механи́ческий, 'mechanical'; механиза́ция, 'mechanization'
-ал-из-ац-ия [30+]		инду́стрия, 'industry'; индустриализа́ция, 'industrialization'
-иц-ия [20+]		компози́тор, 'a composer'; компози́ция, 'a composition'
-и-фик-ац-ия [15+]		ру́сский, 'Russian'; русифика́ция, 'Russification'
-ат-из-ац-ия [10+]		дра́ма, 'drama'; драматиза́ция, 'dramatization'
-ар-из-ац-ия [5+]		соли́дный, 'solid, reliable'; солидариза́ция, 'showing solidarity, making common cause'
-К- [280+/20+] (WP)	I	кова́ть, 'to forge'; ко́вкий, 'malleable'
	II	вяза́ть, 'to knit, tie'; вя́зкий, 'swampy, miry'
	II	ре́зать, 'to cut'; ре́зкий, 'sharp'
-ец-к- [10+]		не́мец, 'a German'; неме́цкий, 'German'
-ниц-к- [5+]		рабо́тник, 'a workman'; рабо́тницкий, 'a workman's'
-щиц-к- (-чиц-) [5+]		прика́зчик, 'a steward'; прика́зчицкий, 'a steward's'
*-К-А [3700+/1100+] (VP)	I	арти́ст, 'an artiste, actor'; арти́стка, 'an artiste, actress'
	I	англича́нин, 'an Englishman'; англича́нка, 'an Englishwoman'
	I	ву́зовец, 'a man student receiving tertiary education'; ву́зовка, 'a woman student'
	II	записа́ть (*Pf.*), 'to note down'; запи́ска, 'a note' (P)
	III	вишнёвый, 'cherry'; вишнёвка, 'cherry brandy' (P)
	III	овся́ный, 'oat, oaten'; овся́нка, 'porridge, oatmeal' (WP)
	IV	чи́стить, 'to clean'; чи́стка, 'cleaning, a purge' (P)
	IV	обмо́лвиться, 'to make a mistake in speaking'; обмо́лвка, 'a slip of the tongue' (P)
	V	задвига́ть (*Ipf.*), 'to push into, bolt'; задви́жка, 'a bolt' (P)
	VI	бе́лый, 'white'; бе́лка, 'a squirrel' (NP)
	VI	ры́жий, 'red, ginger'; Ры́жка (a pet name for a red dog) (NP)

	VII	вы́скочить (*Pf.*), 'to spring out'; вы́скочка, 'an upstart' (NP)
-ан-к-а	I	грек, 'a Greek'; греча́нка, 'a Greek woman'
(-ян-) [200+]	II	сму́глый, 'swarthy, dark'; смугля́нка, 'a dark woman'
-л-к-а [200+]		зажига́ть, 'to light, kindle'; зажига́лка, 'a cigarette lighter'
-ист-к-а [180+]		тури́зм, 'tourism'; тури́стка, 'a tourist' (*f.*)
-ов-к-а (-ев-, -ёв-) [150+]		сверли́ть, 'to bore holes'; сверло́вка, 'the process of boring'
-ин^2-к-а [120+]		песо́к, 'sand'; песчи́нка, 'a grain of sand'
-ант-к-а [30+]		кварти́ра, 'a flat'; соквартира́нтка, 'a flatmate' (*f.*)
-ен^0-к-а (-ён-) [30+]		бе́женец, 'a refugee' (*m.*); бе́женка, 'a refugee' (*f.*)
		францу́з, 'a Frenchman'; францу́женка, 'a Frenchwoman'
		мона́х, 'a monk'; мона́шенка, 'a nun'
-ич-к-а [30+]		алкого́лик, 'an alcoholic' (*m.*); алкого́личка, 'an alcoholic' (*f.*)
-ч^0-ат^1-к-а [20+]		взры́вчатый, 'explosive'; взрывча́тка, 'an explosive'
-яч-к-а [20+]		сибиря́к, 'a Siberian' (*m.*); сибиря́чка, 'a Siberian' (*f.*)
-ёр-к-а [15+]		стаж, 'a period of study or work'; стажёрка, 'a temporary student or worker' (*f.*)
-ий-к-а [15+]		Австра́лия, 'Australia'; австрали́йка, 'an Australian' (*f.*)
-ион-ист-к-а [15+]		импрессиони́зм, 'impressionism'; импрессиони́стка, 'an impressionist' (*f.*)
-ар-к-а [10+]		дика́рь, 'a savage' (*m.*); дика́рка, 'a savage' (*f.*)
-ач-к-а [10+]		рыба́к, 'a fisherman'; рыба́чка, 'a fisherwoman'
-ёж-к-а [10+]		бомби́ть, 'to bomb'; бомбёжка, 'an air-raid, bombardment'
-ион-ер-к-а [10+]		револю́ция, 'a revolution'; революционе́рка, 'a revolutionary' (*f.*)
-ент-к-а [5+]		конкури́ровать, 'to compete'; конкуре́нтка, 'a competitor' (*f.*)
-ин^1-к-а [5+]		Мордва́ (a Finnish people); мордви́нка, 'a Mordvin' (*f.*)

КВАЗИ- [5+] (P)	I специали́ст, 'a specialist'; квазиспециали́ст, 'a self-styled specialist'
-К-О [?] (NP)	I вороно́й, 'black' (of horses); воронко́, 'a black horse'
КОНТР- (КОНТРА-) [60+] (P)	I ме́ра, 'a measure'; контрме́ра, 'a counter-measure'
-Л- [200+/5+] (WP)	I вя́нуть, 'to fade, wither'; вя́лый, 'flabby, dull' I запоте́ть, 'to mist over' (of glass); запоте́лый, 'misted'
-ен-е-л- [5+]	лёд, 'ice'; заледене́лый, 'ice-covered'
-Л-А [20+] (WP)	I запева́ть, 'to lead singing'; запева́ла, 'the leader of a choir'
-ЛИВ- [150+] (P)	*I берегу́ (бере́чь), 'to guard, preserve'; бережли́вый, 'thrifty' I пуга́ть, 'to frighten'; пугли́вый, 'timid' I за́висть (*f.*), 'envy'; зави́стливый, 'envious'
-Л-О [70+] (WP)	I бить, 'to beat'; би́ло, 'an instrument used for beating, striking' I пра́вить, 'to guide'; пра́вило, 'a rule'
-ЛЬ [5+] (WP)	I врать, 'to tell fibs, exaggerate'; враль (*m.*), 'a fibber, man fond of telling tall stories' See also -ТЕЛЬ
-М- (-ЕМ-, -ОМ-) [250+] (P)	I выноси́ть, 'to endure'; невыноси́мый, 'unbearable' I жела́ть, 'to wish'; жела́емый, 'desirable' I соедини́ть, 'to combine, compound'; соедини́мый, 'able to enter into compounds'
МАКРО- [20+] (P)	I фотосъёмка, 'photography'; макрофотосъёмка, 'large-scale photography'
МЕЖ- (МЕЖДУ-) [80+] (P)	I плане́та, 'a planet'; межплане́тный, 'interplanetary, space' I зубно́й, 'dental'; межзу́бный, 'interdental' I го́род, 'a town'; междугоро́дный, 'interurban'
МИКРО- [70+] (P)	I части́ца, 'a particle'; микрочасти́ца, 'a microparticle'

МИМО- [5+] (NP)	I	лёт, 'flight'; мимолётный, 'passing, transient'
-Н^{1}- [3900+/2500+] (VP)	I	боло́то, 'a marsh'; боло́тный, 'marsh'
	II	спор, 'a dispute'; спо́рный, 'disputed, open to argument'
	II	семья́, 'a family'; семе́йный, 'family' (P)
	III	заме́тить, 'to notice'; заме́тный, 'perceptible' (P)
	III	слы́шать, 'to hear'; неслы́шный, 'inaudible' (P)
-тель-н^{1}- [720+]	I	удовлетвори́ть, 'to satisfy'; удовлетвори́тельный, 'satisfactory'
	II	употреби́ть, 'to use'; употреби́тельный, 'in common use'
	III	осуши́ть, 'to dry, drain'; осуши́тельный кана́л, 'a drainage canal'
-оч-н^{1}- (-еч-) [500+]		доба́вить, 'to add'; доба́вочный, 'additional'
		брусо́к, 'a small beam, a bar'; брусо́чный, 'relating to a брусо́к'
-ич-н^{1}- [270+]		мело́дия, 'a melody'; мелоди́чный, 'melodious'
-аль-н^{1}- [180+]		геоме́трия, 'geometry'; геометра́льный, 'geometrical'
-ль-н^{1}- [140+]		купа́ться, 'to bathe'; купа́льный, 'bathing'
		ме́рить, 'to measure'; мери́льный, 'measuring'
-ив-н^{1}- [130+]		федера́ция, 'a federation'; федерати́вный, 'federative'
-ац-ион-н^{1}- (-яц-) [80+]		обсервато́рия, 'an observatory'; обсерваци-о́нный, 'observational'
-ин-н^{1}- [80+]		равни́на, 'a plain'; равни́нный, 'relating to a plain'
-иаль-н^{1}- [50+]		мате́рия, 'matter'; материа́льный, 'material'
-ар-н^{1}- (-яр-) [40+]		плане́та, 'a planet'; планета́рный, 'planetary'
-оз^{0}-н^{1}- [40+]		рели́гия, 'religion'; религио́зный, 'religious'
-ост-н^{1}- [40+]		сла́дкий, 'sweet'; сла́достный, 'delicious, sweet' (*Poet.*)
		пове́рхность (*f.*), 'surface'; пове́рхностный, 'superficial'
-еб-н^{1}- [30+]		суд, 'a court'; суде́бный, 'judicial'

-ий-н^{1}- [30+]	корро́зия, ‘corrosion’; коррози́йный, ‘corrosion’
-ион-аль-н^{1}- [20+]	се́кция, ‘a section’; секциона́льный, ‘sectional’
-ион-н^{1}- [20+]	телеви́зия (= телеви́дение), ‘television’; телевизио́нный, ‘television’
-ат-ор-н^{1}- [15+]	генера́ция, ‘generation’; генера́тор, ‘a generator’; генера́торный, ‘relating to a генера́тор’
-ов^{2}-н^{1}- (-ев-) [15+]	дух, ‘spirit’; духо́вный, ‘spiritual’
-ур-н^{1}- [15+]	архитекту́ра, ‘architecture’; архитекту́рный, ‘architectural’
-абель-н^{1}- [10+]	комфо́рт, ‘comfort’; комфорта́бельный, ‘comfortable’
-из-ац-ион-н^{1}- [10+]	коло́ния, ‘a colony’; колонизацио́нный, ‘colonization’
-уаль^{0}-н^{1}- [10+]	индиви́д, ‘an individual’; индивидуа́льный, ‘individual’
-аж^{0}-н^{1}- [5+]	карто́н, ‘cardboard’; картона́жный, ‘made of cardboard’
-в-н^{1}- [5+]	держа́ва, ‘a state, power’; великодержа́вный, ‘great-power’
-ель-н^{1}- [5+]	смерть (*f.*), ‘death’; смерте́льный, ‘fatal’ ги́бель (*f.*), ‘destruction’; ги́бельный, ‘ruinous’
-ес-н^{1}- [5+]	не́бо, ‘sky, heaven’; небе́сный, ‘celestial’
-ёж-н^{1}- [5+]	молодо́й, ‘young’; молодёжный, ‘young people’s’
-иц-ион-н^{1}- [5+]	реквизи́ровать, ‘to requisition’; реквизицио́нный, ‘requisition’
-ищ-н^{1}- [5+]	учи́лище, ‘a school’; учи́лищный, ‘school’
-Н^{2}- (-ЕН-, -ЁН-) [120+] (NP)	I дать, ‘to give’; дарёный, ‘given’ (cf. дарёному коню́ в зу́бы не смо́трят) I жа́рить, ‘to fry’; жа́реная карто́шка, ‘fried potatoes, chips’ I ждать, ‘to wait, expect’; нежда́ный, ‘unexpected’
-Н-А (*Suffix not found alone*) [0/?]	See -Н^{1}-, -ИН^{1}
-ин^{1}-ич-н-а [?]	Илья́ (the Christian name Il’ya); Ильи́нична (the patronymic ‘daughter of Il’ya’)
-ич-н-а [?]	Ники́та (the Christian name Nikita); Ники́тична (the patronymic ‘daughter of Nikita’)

-ов-н-а (-ев-) [?]		Дми́трий (the Christian name Dmitri); Дми́триевна (the patronymic 'daughter of Dmitri')
НА- (*verbal*) [900+]		бежа́ть, 'to run'; набежа́ть, 'to run upon, against'; набе́г, 'an invasion, raid' расти́, 'to grow'; нарасти́, 'to swell, increase'; наро́ст, 'a growth, excrescence'; нараще́ние, 'augmentation'
НА- [10+] (P)	I I	стол, 'a table'; насто́льная кни́га, 'a reference book' грудь (*f.*), 'breast, chest'; нагру́дник, 'a child's bib'
НАД- (*verbal*) [100+]		лома́ть/ломи́ть, 'to break'; надломи́ть, 'to crack'; надло́м, 'a crack' стро́ить, 'to build'; надстро́ить, 'to build on top, to build more'; надстро́йка, 'superstructure'
НАД- [40+] (P)	I	строка́, 'a line of writing, print'; надстро́чные зна́ки, 'diacritics'
НАИ- [5+] (WP)	I	лу́чший, 'better'; наилу́чший, 'best'
НЕ- [300+/770+] (P)	I II	весёлый, 'merry, happy'; невесёлый, 'subdued, sad' пого́да, 'weather'; непого́да, 'bad weather' (NP)
не-до- [120+]		де́лать, 'to make'; недоде́ланный, 'unfinished'
не-у- [120+]		уда́ться, 'to turn out well'; неуда́чный, 'unsuccessful'
не-о- (-об-) [90+]		обде́лать, 'to finish, round off'; необде́ланный, 'rough, unfinished' описа́ть, 'to describe'; неопи́санный, 'not previously described'
не-из- [60+]		лечи́ть, 'to heal'; неизлечи́мый, 'incurable'
не-по- [60+]		ме́ра, 'a measure'; непоме́рный, 'excessive' пода́ть, 'to give, yield'; непода́тливый, 'unyielding'
не-при- [50+]		приступа́ть, 'to approach, begin'; непристу́пный, 'unapproachable, inaccessible'
не-раз- (-рас-) [50+]		разбира́ть, 'to sort out, analyse'; неразбо́рчивый, 'undecipherable'

не-за- [40+]	заинтересоваться, 'to become interested'; незаинтересо́ванный, 'not involved, interested'
не-со- [30+]	разме́р, 'a dimension'; несоразме́рный, 'unsymmetrical, incommensurate'
не-воз- (вос-) [20+]	возбуди́ть, 'to arouse'; невозбуди́мый, 'indifferent to stimuli'
не-вы- [20+]	выноси́ть, 'to bear'; невыноси́мый, 'unbearable'
не-на- [20+]	наказа́ть, 'to punish'; ненаказу́емый, 'non-punishable'
не-про- [20+]	проника́ть, 'to penetrate'; непроница́емый, 'impermeable'
не-без- [15+]	интере́сный, 'interesting'; небезынтере́сный, 'quite interesting'
не-от- [15+]	отложи́ть, 'to postpone'; неотло́жный, 'immediate'
не-под- [15+]	подде́лать, 'to imitate, forge'; неподде́льный, 'authentic'
не-пре- [15+]	прерыва́ть, 'to interrupt'; непреры́вный, 'uninterrupted'
не-в- [5+]	меша́ть, 'to interrupt, hinder'; невмеша́тельство, 'non-interference'
не-до-вы- [5+]	вы́полнить, 'to fulfil'; недовыполне́ние, 'under-fulfilment'
не-пред-у- [5+]	умы́слить, 'to plot'; непредумы́шленный, 'unpremeditated'
НЕО- [50+] (P)	I романти́зм, 'romanticism'; неоромanти́зм, 'neo-romanticism'
-Н-ИЕ	See -ЬЕ
НИЗ- (НИС-) (*verbal*) [10+]	положи́ть, 'to lay'; низложи́ть, 'to depose'; низложе́ние, 'deposition, casting down'
-НИК† [850+/360+] (P)	I по́мощь (*f.*), 'help, assistance'; помо́щник, 'an assistant, helper'
	I рабо́тать, 'to work'; рабо́тник, 'a workman' (NP)
	I отойти́, 'to go away'; отше́льник, 'a hermit' (NP)
	II гра́дус, 'a degree' (in measurement); гра́дусник, 'a thermometer' (WP)
	II пыль (*f.*), 'dust, pollen'; пы́льник, 'a dustcoat, duster; an anther' (WP)

† See footnote to -ИК.

	II	поднять, 'to lift'; подъём, 'the act of lifting'; подъёмник, 'an automatic lift' (WP)
	III	салат, 'salad, lettuce'; салатник, 'a salad bowl' (WP)
	III	пчела, 'a bee'; пчельник, 'a beehive' (WP)
	*III	бумага, 'paper, a note'; бумажник, 'a wallet' (WP)
	IV	крапива, 'nettles'; крапивник, 'a bed of nettles' (WP)
	V	окно, 'a window'; подоконник, 'a window-sill' (WP)
	V	ухо, 'an ear'; уши, 'ears'; наушники, 'ear-phones' (WP)
		N.B. In III mutation only occasional.
-ль^{0}-ник [100+]		холодить, 'to cool'; холодильник, 'a refrigerator'
		умываться, 'to get washed'; умывальник, 'a washbasin'
-оч-ник (-еч-) [100+]	I	стачка, 'a strike'; стачечник, 'a striker'
	II	конец, 'an end, the end'; наконечник, 'a tip, the end of some object'
	II	солнце, 'the sun'; подсолнечник, 'a sunflower'
-н-ник (-ен-) [80+]		воспитать, 'to bring up'; воспитанник, 'a ward, a student'
-ов^{2}-ник (-ев-) [50+]	I	день, 'a day'; дневник, 'a diary'
	II	баловать, 'to spoil'; баловник, 'a spoilt child, a capricious person'
-ят-ник [15+]		цыплята, 'chickens'; цыплятник, 'a dealer in chickens; a hawk preying on chickens'
		соболь (*m.*), 'a sable'; соболятник, 'a sable trapper'
-ин-ник [10+]	I	дружина, 'a bodyguard, brigade of vigilantes'; дружинник, 'a vigilante'
	II	смородина, 'currants'; смородинник, 'a cluster of currant bushes'
-еб-ник [5+]		служба, 'service, a service'; служебник, 'a missal'
*-НИЦ-А† [350+/220+] (P)	I	бог, 'God, a God'; безбожница, 'an atheist' (*f.*)
	I	работать, 'to work'; работница, 'a woman worker'
	II	молоть, мелю, 'to grind'; мельница, 'a mill' (NP)
	III	сахар, 'sugar'; сахарница, 'a sugar basin' (WP)
		Compare -НИК (I, II, III) and see also -ИЦ-А

† See footnote to -ИЦ-А.

Suffix	Class	Examples
-тель-ниц-а (-итель-) [150+]		учи́тель, 'a teacher' (*m.*); учи́тельница, 'a teacher' (*f.*)
-н-ниц-а (-ен-) [30+]		путеше́ствовать, 'to travel'; путеше́ственница, 'a traveller' (*f.*)
-еб-ниц-а [10+]		лече́бный, 'medical'; лече́бница, 'a spa, health resort'
-ов^2-ниц-а [10+]		сад, 'a garden'; садо́вница, 'a gardener' (*f.*)
-ль-ниц-а [5+]		мы́ло, 'soap'; мы́льница, 'a soap-dish'
-оч-ниц-а [5+]		взя́тка, 'a bribe'; взя́точница, 'a bribe-taker' (*f.*)
-НН- (-ЕНН-, -ЁНН-) [450+/10+] (P)	I	смири́ть, 'to subdue'; смирённый, 'subdued'
	I	сдержа́ть, 'to restrain'; сде́ржанный, 'restrained'
		See also -ЕНН-
-з-ова-нн- [10+]		центра́льный, 'central'; централизо́ванный, 'centralized'
-НЬ- [100+/20+] (WP)	I	весна́, 'spring'; весе́нний, 'spring, vernal'
	II	дочь, 'a daughter' (stem = дочер-); доче́рний, 'daughter's' (NP)
	II	сын, 'a son'; сыно́вний, 'son's, filial' (NP)
-ш^0-нь- [20+]		вчера́, 'yesterday'; вчера́шний, 'yesterday's'
-Н-Я [160+/80+] (WP)	I	паха́ть (пашу́), 'to plough'; па́шня, 'a ploughed field'
	I	ко́фе (originally ко́фей), 'coffee'; кофе́йня, 'a café'
	I	гонча́р, 'a potter'; гонча́рня, 'a pottery' (NP)
	II	вози́ться, 'to fuss, busy oneself'; возня́, 'noise, a fuss'
-ль-н-я [60+]		раздева́ться, 'to undress'; раздева́льня, 'a cloakroom'
-от-н-я [20+]		шёпот, 'a whisper'; шепотня́, 'a whispering'
О-, ОБ- (ОБО-, ОБЪ-) (*verbal*) [1500+/50+]		ка́мень (*m.*), 'stone'; окамене́ть, 'to turn to stone, stiffen'; окамене́ние, 'petrifaction'
		кра́сить, 'to paint'; окра́сить, 'to paint, touch up'; окра́ска, 'the act of painting; a hue'
		хвати́ть/схвати́ть, 'to grasp'; охвати́ть, 'to envelop, surround'; охва́т, 'scope'
		е́хать, 'to travel'; объе́хать, 'to make a detour; to tour'; объе́зд, 'a detour; a tour, long ride'

		писа́ть, ‘to write’; описа́ть, ‘to describe’; описа́ние, ‘a description’
		писа́ть, ‘to write’; описа́ться, ‘to make a mistake in writing’; опи́ска, ‘a slip of the pen’
		суди́ть, ‘to judge’; осуди́ть, ‘to condemn’; осужде́ние, ‘blame, censure’
о-без- (-бес-) [40+]		жир, ‘fat’; обезжи́ренный, ‘fatless, skimmed’
о-по- [5+]		позна́ть, ‘to get to know’; опо́знанный, ‘recognized, identified’
о-про- [5+]		ки́нуть, ‘to throw’; опроки́нутый, ‘overturned, capsized’
О- [10+] (WP)	I	ше́я, ‘a neck’; оше́йник, ‘an animal’s collar’
-ОБ-А [10+] (NP]	I I	злой, ‘bad, angry’; зло́ба, ‘malice, spite’ стыд, ‘shame’; стыдо́ба (*Pop.*), ‘shame’
-ОВ^{1} (-ЕВ) [?] (P)	I I II III	внук, ‘a grandson’; вну́ков, ‘grandson’s’ козёл, ‘a goat’; козло́в, ‘belonging to one goat in particular’ (NP) Пётр (the Christian name Peter); Петро́в (the surname Petrov); Петро́ва, ‘the wife of Petrov’ (WP) песо́к, ‘sand’; Псков (the town of Pskov) (WP)
-ОВ^{2}- (-ЕВ-) [780+/270+] (VP)	I II	тюль (*m.*), ‘tulle’; тю́левые за́навески, ‘lace curtains’ де́ло, ‘an affair, business’; делово́й челове́к, ‘a businessman’
-к-ов^{0}- [150+]		уча́сток, ‘a plot, area’; участко́вый, ‘relating to an уча́сток’ ко́рка, ‘a crust, rind’; ко́рковый, ‘relating to a ко́рка’
-ин^{3}-ов^{0}- [30+]		сахари́н, ‘saccharine’; сахари́новый, ‘relating to сахари́н’
-ик-ов^{0}- [20+]		тупи́к, ‘a blind alley’; тупико́вый, ‘relating to a тупи́к’
-ит^{2}-ов^{0}- [20+]		малахи́т, ‘malachite’; малахи́товый, ‘made of malachite’
-ник-ов^{0}- [20+]		ледни́к, ‘a glacier’; леднико́вый, ‘relating to a ледни́к’
-ц-ов^{0}- (-ев-) [20+]	I II	свине́ц, ‘lead’; свинцо́вый, ‘made of lead’ дворе́ц, ‘a palace’; дворцо́вый переворо́т, ‘a palace revolution’

-н-ев^{0}- [5+]		греча, 'buckwheat'; гре́чневый, 'buckwheat'
-як-ов^{0}- [5+]		пустяки́, 'trifles'; пустяко́вый, 'trivial'
-ОВ-О [?] (WP)	I I	внук, 'a grandson'; Вну́ков (the surname Vnukov); Вну́ково (the suburb of Vnukovo) Фрол (the Christian name Frol, Florus); Фро́лово (the village of (St.) Frol)
-ОВО [?] (NP)	I	сухо́й, 'dry'; Сухово́ (the surname Sukhovo)
-ОК (-ЕК) [350+/60+] (WP)	I II III IV	зева́ть, 'to yawn'; зево́к, 'a yawn' обломи́ть, 'to break off'; обло́мок, 'a fragment' ше́я, 'a neck'; переше́ек, 'an isthmus' де́сять, 'ten'; деся́ток, 'a set of ten' (NP)
-ён-ок (-он-) [60+]		волк, 'a wolf'; волчо́нок, 'a wolf cub'
-ОМ-		See -М-
-ОР (*Isol. only*) [60+/160+]	I	агре́ссия, 'aggression'; агре́ссор, 'an aggressor'
-ат-ор (-ят-) [110+]		изоли́ровать, 'to isolate, insulate'; изоля́тор, 'an insulator; a prison'
-из-ат-ор [30+]		катало́г, 'a catalogue'; каталогиза́тор, 'a cataloguer'
-ит-ор [10+]		инквизи́ция, 'an inquisition'; инквизи́тор, 'an inquisitor'
-фик-ат-ор [10+]		кодифици́ровать, 'to codify'; кодифика́тор, 'a codifier'
-ОСТЬ (-ЕСТЬ) [100+/2360+] (VP)	I I	све́жий, 'fresh'; све́жесть, 'freshness' рад, 'happy'; ра́дость, 'happiness, joy'
-н^{1}-ость [800+]		абсолю́тный, 'absolute'; абсолю́тность, 'absoluteness'
-нн-ость (-енн-, -ённ-) [400+]		преда́ться, 'to devote oneself'; пре́данность, 'devotion'
-тель-н^{1}-ость [240+]	I II	расти́, 'to grow'; расти́тельность, 'vegetation' впечатле́ние, 'an impression'; впечатли́тельность, 'impressionability'
-м-ость (-ем-) [200+]		воспламеня́ть, 'to set alight'; воспламеня́емость, 'inflammability'

-ич-н^{1}-ость [120+]
категóрия, ‘a category’; категори́чность, ‘categorical nature’

-лив-ость [100+]
терпе́ть, ‘to bear, endure’; терпели́вость, ‘patience’

-ист-ость [80+]
ветвь (*f.*), ‘a branch, twig’; ветви́стость, ‘branching, ramification’

-к-ость [70+]
ги́бкий, ‘flexible’; ги́бкость, ‘flexibility’

-л-ость [70+]
устаре́ть, ‘to grow old’; устаре́лость, ‘obsolescence’

-аль-н^{1}-ость [50+]
мате́рия, ‘matter’; материа́льность, ‘materiality, material considerations’

-ив-н^{1}-ость [50+]
прогре́сс, ‘progress’; прогресси́вность, ‘progressiveness’

-чив-ость [50+]
нахóдчивый, ‘resourceful’; нахóдчивость, ‘resourcefulness’

-ов^{2}-ат^{1}-ость [30+]
сырóй, ‘raw’; сыровáтость, ‘the quality of being rather raw’

-ий-н^{1}-ость [10+]
пáртия, ‘a political party’; парти́йность, ‘party-mindedness’

-ов^{2}-ость [10+]
план, ‘a plan’; плáновость, ‘planning, the principle of planning’

-оз-н^{1}-ость [10+]
рели́гия, ‘religion’; религиóзность, ‘religiosity’

-ост-н^{1}-ость [10+]
це́лостный, ‘complete’; це́лостность, ‘completeness’

-уч-есть [10+]
певу́чий, ‘melodious’; певу́честь, ‘melodiousness’

-ч^{0}-ат^{1}-ость [10+]
взрывáть, ‘to explode’; взры́вчатость, ‘explosiveness’

-яв-ость (-ав-) [10+]
вели́чие, ‘grandeur’; величáвость, ‘imposing appearance’

-абель-н^{1}-ость [5+]
респе́кт (= уваже́ние), ‘respect’; респектáбельность, ‘respectability’

-ар-н^{1}-ость [5+]
элеме́нт, ‘an element’; элементáрность, ‘elementary nature, importance’

-ляв-ость [5+]
верте́ть, ‘to turn’; вертля́вость, ‘inability to keep still’

-н^{2}-ость [5+]
учи́ть, ‘to teach, learn’; учёность, ‘erudition’

-ов^{2}-ит^{4}-ость [5+]
дарови́тый, ‘talented’; дарови́тость, ‘the possession of talent’

-ов^{2}-н^{1}-ость [5+]
винá, ‘a fault, guilt’; винóвность, ‘culpability’

ОТ-
(*verbal*)
[800+]

звуча́ть, 'to sound'; отзвуча́ть, 'to die away' (of sounds); о́тзвук, 'a faint, dying sound, an echo'
крыть, 'to cover'; откры́ть, 'to uncover, discover'; откры́тие, 'a discovery'
шлифова́ть, 'to polish'; отшлифова́ть, 'to rub perfectly smooth'; отшлифо́вка (this action)
пра́вить, 'to drive, steer'; отпра́вить, 'to send off'; отпра́вка, 'consignment, sending away'

ОТ-

I глаго́л, 'a verb'; отглаго́льный, 'deverbal, deverbative'

-ОТ
[10+]
(NP)

I то́пать, 'to stamp one's foot'; то́пот, 'a tramping, a clatter of hooves'
I гро́хнуть (*Pf.*), 'to drop something noisily'; гро́хот, 'a crash'

-ОТ-А
(-ЕТ-)
[80+]
(NP)

I по́лный, 'full'; полнота́, 'plenitude, completeness'
I срам, 'shame'; срамота́ (*Pop.*), 'shame'
II рвать (его́ рвёт), 'to vomit'; рво́та, 'vomiting; vomit'

-ОТЬ
[5+]
(NP)

I копти́ть, 'to smoke, cover with smoke'; ко́поть (*f.*), 'grime'

-ОХ-А
(-ЁХ-)
[10+]
(NP)

I опи́ться (*Pf.*), 'to become extremely drunk'; опиво́ха (*Pop.*), 'an alcoholic'
I пройти́ (*Pf.*) (он пройдёт), 'to go through, pass'; пройдо́ха (*Pop.*), 'a cunning man'

ПАН-
[20+]
(WP)

I герма́нский, 'German'; пангерма́нский, 'pan-German'; пангермани́зм, 'pan-Germanism'
I славя́не, 'the Slavs'; панслави́зм, 'pan-Slavism'
I теи́зм, 'theism'; пантеи́зм, 'pantheism'

ПЕРЕ-
(*verbal*)
[750+/40+]

пра́вить, 'to drive, steer'; перепра́вить, 'to send across'; перепра́ва, 'a ferry, a ford'
стро́ить, 'to build'; перестро́ить, 'to rebuild, alter'; перестро́йка, 'reconstruction'
жить, 'to live'; пережи́ть, 'to outlive, survive; to experience'; пережи́ток, 'a survival, remnant'; пережива́ние, 'an experience'
брани́ть, 'to scold'; перебра́ниваться (*Ipf.*), 'to squabble with'; перебра́нка, 'a heated exchange'

пере-о^{0}-
[15+]

охлади́ть, 'to cool'; переохлажде́ние, 'supercooling'

пере-за-
[10+]

заключи́ть, 'to conclude, arrange'; перезаключе́ние, 'renewal of an agreement, arrangement'

пере-у- [10+]	устро́ить, 'to arrange'; переустро́енный, 're-arranged'
пере-про- [5+]	прове́рить, 'to check'; перепрове́рка, 'a re-check'
ПЕРЕД- (-ПЕРЕДО-, ПЕРЕДЪ-)	See ПРЕД-
ПО- (*verbal*) [1300+]	бежа́ть, 'to run'; побежа́ть, 'to start running; to reach by running'; побе́г, 'an escape; a fresh shoot, sprout' ка́шлять, 'to cough'; пока́шливать, 'to cough lightly and repeatedly'; пока́шливание, 'a light, repeated coughing' лома́ть (*Ipf.*), 'to break'; полома́ть (*Pf.*), 'to break; to break several objects'; поло́мка, 'a defect; breakage(s)' (cf. штраф за поло́мку, 'a fine for breakages')
ПО- [100+] (P)	I ме́сяц, 'a month'; поме́сячный, 'monthly' II дохо́д, 'an income'; подохо́дный, 'according to one's income' II си́ла, 'strength'; непоси́льный, 'beyond one's strength, not according to one's strength' III мо́ре, 'the sea'; помо́рье, 'a coastal district' (WP) III грани́ца, 'a frontier'; пограни́чный, 'border, along the frontier'; пограни́чник, 'a frontier guard' (WP) IV смерть (*f.*), 'death'; посме́ртный, 'posthumous' (WP)
ПОД- (ПОДО-, ПОДЪ-) (*verbal*) [750+/10+]	держа́ть, 'to hold'; поддержа́ть, 'to support'; подде́ржка, 'support' лить, 'to pour'; подли́ть, 'to add' (a liquid); подли́вка, 'addition of a liquid, an added liquid' жа́рить, 'to fry, grill'; поджа́рить, 'to fry, grill lightly'; поджа́рка (*Pop.*), 'a lightly cooked dish' сказа́ть, 'to say'; подсказа́ть, 'to prompt, say secretively, egg on'; подска́зка, 'prompting; a piece of encouragement'
ПОД- [200+/10+] (P)	I земля́, 'ground'; подзе́мная желе́зная доро́га, 'an underground railway, Metro, tube' I ко́жа, 'skin'; подко́жный, 'hypodermic' II вид, 'a species'; подви́д, 'a sub-species' III го́род, 'a town, city'; подгоро́дный, 'suburban' (WP)

под-за- [5+]		забы́ть, 'to forget'; подзабы́тый, 'half-forgotten' заголо́вок, 'a title'; подзаголо́вок, 'a sub-title'
под-от- [5+]		отде́л, 'a department'; подотде́л, 'a sub-department'
ПОСЛЕ- [15+] (WP)	I	де́йствие, 'an effect'; последе́йствие, 'an after-effect'
ПРЕ- (*verbal*) [100+/20+]		ступи́ть (*Pf.*), 'to step'; преступи́ть, 'to transgress'; преступле́ние, 'a crime' See also ПЕРЕ-
ПРЕ- [30+/30+] (P)	I	заба́вный, 'amusing'; презаба́вный (*Pop.*), 'extremely amusing'
пре-воз- (-вос-) [10+]		восходи́ть, 'to ascend'; превосхо́дный, 'excellent'
пре^{0}-о- [5+]		одоле́ть, 'to overcome'; преодоле́ние, 'victory, mastery'
пре-по^{0}- [5+]		подава́ть, 'to give'; преподава́тель, 'an instructor'
пре-у- [5+]		увели́чить, 'to enlarge'; преувели́чить, 'to exaggerate'
ПРЕД- (ПРЕДЪ-) (*verbal*) [170+/60+]		ви́деть, 'to see'; предви́деть, 'to foresee'; предви́дение, 'foresight' ста́вить, 'to put, stand'; предста́вить, 'to present, offer'; представле́ние, 'a performance; conception; presentation'
пред-о- [15+]		остерега́ть, 'to warn'; предостереже́ние, 'a warning, caution'
пред-у- [15+]		убеди́ть, 'to convince'; предубеждённый, 'prejudiced'
пред-по^{0}- [10+]		положи́ть, 'to place'; предположи́ть, 'to suppose'; предположе́ние, 'a supposition'
пред-воз- (-вос-) [5+]		восхити́ться, 'to admire, be carried away'; предвосхище́ние, 'anticipation'
пред-на- [5+]		начерта́ть, 'to trace out'; предначе́ртанный судьбо́й, 'predestined'
пред-при- [5+]		приня́ть, 'to accept, take'; предприя́тие, 'an undertaking, enterprise'
ПРЕД- [70+/5+] (P)	I	вы́боры, 'elections'; предвы́борный, 'eve-of-election'
	II	гора́, 'a mountain'; предго́рье, 'foothills'

пред-рас- [5+]		рассве́т, 'dawn'; предрассве́тный, 'before the dawn'
ПРИ- (*verbal*) [750+/10+]		е́хать, 'to travel'; прие́хать, 'to arrive'; прие́зд, 'arrival' бли́зиться, 'to draw near'; прибли́зиться (*Pf.*), 'to draw near'; приблизи́тельный, 'approximate'; приближе́ние, 'approach' положи́ть, 'to put, lay'; приложи́ть, 'to append'; приложе́ние, 'a supplement, appended material' теса́ть, 'to hew, trim'; притеса́ть, 'to trim smooth'; притёска, 'smoothing, planing' ту́хнуть, 'to fade away, be extinguished'; приту́хнуть, 'to fail, become faint' (of lights, radio waves); притуха́ние, 'fading, loss of sound or brightness'
при-у- [10+]		уме́ньши́ть, 'to diminish'; приуменьшённый, 'somewhat diminished'
ПРИ- [?] (P)	I I	вокза́л, 'a railway station'; привокза́льный рестора́н, 'a station restaurant' Во́лга, 'the river Volga'; приво́лжский, 'on the banks of the Volga'
ПРО- (*verbal*) [900+/20+]		игра́ть, 'to play'; проигра́ть, 'to lose a game'; про́игрыш, 'a loss, a gambling loss' руби́ть, 'to chop'; проруби́ть, 'to cut through, make a hole'; про́рубь (*f.*), 'an ice-hole' смотре́ть, 'to look'; просмотре́ть, 'to look through, to read through'; просмо́тр, 'a perusal' е́хать, 'to travel'; прое́хать, 'to pass through'; прое́зд, 'a way through; the act of passing through' мо́кнуть, 'to get wet'; промо́кнуть, 'to be thoroughly soaked'; промока́ние, 'a thorough soaking; the act of soaking'
про[1]-из- [20+]		носи́ть, 'to carry'; произноше́ние, 'pronunciation'
про[1]-воз- [5+]		гласи́ть, 'to say, announce'; провозглашённый, 'widely proclaimed'
ПРО- [?] (P)	I	сове́т, 'a Soviet'; просове́тский, 'pro-Soviet'
ПРОТИВО- (*verbal*) [5+]		положи́ть (*Pf.*), 'to put, lay'; противоположи́ть, 'to oppose'; противополо́жный, 'opposite'

Prefix		Examples
ПРОТИВО-	I	вес, 'a weight'; противовéс, 'a counter-weight'
[60+]	I	яд, 'poison'; противоя́дие, 'an antidote'
(P)	I	естéственный, 'natural'; противоестéственный, 'unnatural'
ПСЕВДО- [20+] (P)	I	искýсство, 'art'; псевдоискýсство, 'false art, pseudo-art'
РАЗ- (РАЗО-, РАЗЪ-, РАС-) (*verbal*) [1100+/30+]		рвать, 'to tear'; разрывáть, разорвáть, 'to tear apart; to tear in pieces'; разры́в отношéний, 'a break in a relationship'
		положи́ть (*Pf.*), 'to put, lay'; разложи́ть, 'to distribute'; разложи́ться, 'to disintegrate'; разложéние, 'distribution, disintegration'
		мáзать, 'to smear'; размáзать, 'to smear all over a surface'; размáзка (*Pop.*) (this action)
		вить, 'to weave, twist'; разви́ть, 'to develop' (*trans.*); разви́тие, 'development, evolution'
		очаровáть, 'to charm'; разочаровáть, 'to disillusion'; разочаровáние, 'disillusionment'
рас-по- [15+]		познавáть, 'to get to know'; распознавáние, 'a diagnosis'
рас-про- [10+]	I	прокля́сть, 'to curse'; распрокля́тый, 'most damned, accursed'
	II	простерéть, 'to extend, reach out'; распростёртый, 'outspread'
раз-у- [10+]		убрáть, 'to decorate'; разýбранный, 'decked out, heavily adorned'
РАС-		See РАЗ-
С- (СО-) (*verbal*) [1700+/30+]		бли́зкий, 'close'; сбли́зить, 'to bring together'; сближéние, 'a rapprochement; intimacy'
		пускáть, 'to release'; спускáть (*Ipf.*), 'to lower, let down'; спуск, 'a lowering, descent; a slope'
		рéзать, 'to cut'; срéзать, 'to cut off'; срéзок, 'a detached piece'
		прáвить, 'to drive, guide'; спрáвить, 'to carry out *successfully*'; спрáвиться, 'to cope'; спрáвка, 'information'
		держáть, 'to hold'; сдержáть поры́в, 'to manage to control an impulse'; сдéржанность, 'self-control'
		See also СО-
со-в- [15+]		помести́ть, 'to place, locate'; совмести́мый, 'compatible'
с-на- [5+]		ряди́ться, 'to dress up'; снаряжéние, 'equipment, harness'

со-от-
[5+]

относи́тельный, 'relative'; соотноси́тельный, 'correlative'

со-по^{0}-
[5+]

поста́вить, 'to stand, place'; сопоста́вленный, 'compared, confronted'

со^{0}-при-
[5+]

косну́ться, 'to touch'; соприкоснове́ние, 'contact'

САМ-О-
[300+]
(P)

I служи́ть, 'to serve'; обслужи́ть, 'to serve, service'; самообслу́живание, 'self-service'
I грузи́ть, 'to load'; разгружа́ть (*Ipf.*), 'to unload'; саморазгружа́ющийсяваго́н, 'a hopper'

СВЕРХ-
[60+]
(P)

I ме́ра, 'a measure'; сверхме́рный, 'excessive'
I челове́к, 'a person'; сверхчелове́к, 'a superman'
II ни́зкий, 'low'; сверхни́зкая температу́ра, 'an extremely low temperature' (WP)

*-СК-
(*-ЕСК-)
(-ЦК-)
[750+/1730+]
(VP)

I Кита́й, 'China'; кита́йский, 'Chinese'
I го́род, 'a town'; городско́й, 'urban' (P)
*I Во́лга (the river Volga); во́лжский, 'Volga' (P)
*I каба́к, 'a public house'; каба́цкий, 'public-house' (NP)
I Нью Йорк, 'New York'; нью-йо́ркский, 'of New York' (P)
*I чех, 'a Czech'; че́шский, 'Czech' (WP)
*I друг, 'a friend'; дру́жеский, 'friendly, amicable' (WP)
*I патриа́рх, 'a Patriarch'; патриа́ршеский, 'Patriarchal' (WP)
*I князь (*m.*), 'a prince'; кня́жеский, 'prince's, princely' (WP)
*I оте́ц, 'a father'; оте́ческий, 'paternal' (WP)

-ич-еск-
[1050+]

биоло́гия, 'biology'; биологи́ческий, 'biological'
те́хника, 'technology, technical science, technique'; техни́ческий, 'technical'
социали́ст, 'a socialist'; социалисти́ческий, 'socialist'

-ист-ск-
[130+]

тури́зм, 'tourism'; тури́стский, 'tourist's'

-ч^{0}-еск-
[100+]

языкове́дение, 'linguistics'; языкове́дческий, 'relating to linguistics'

-тель-ск-
[90+]

вымога́тель, 'an extortioner, blackmailer'; вымога́тельский, 'extortioner's; extortionate'

-ов^{1}-ск-
(-ев-, -ёв-)
[50+]

Кремль (*m.*), 'the Kremlin'; кремлёвский, 'Kremlin'

-ов^{2}-ск- (-ев-, -ёв-) [50+]		банк, ‘a bank’; ба́нковский, ‘bank’
-ей^{0}-ск- [40+]		а́рмия, ‘an army’; арме́йский, ‘army’
-ан^{0}-ск- [30+]		Аме́рика, ‘America’; америка́нский, ‘American’
-ат-ор-ск- [30+]		консервати́зм, ‘conservatism’; консервато́рский, ‘possessed by a conservative’
-ант-ск- [20+]		эмигра́ция, ‘emigration’; эмигра́нтский, ‘emigrant’
-ен^{0}-ч-еск- [20+]		младе́нец, ‘an infant’; младе́нческий, ‘infantile’
-ёр-ск- [20+]		дирижи́ровать, ‘to conduct a choir or orchestra’; дирижёрский, ‘conductor’s’
-ий^{0}-ск- [20+]		Ла́твия, ‘Latvia’; латви́йский, ‘Latvian’ А́льпы, ‘the Alps’; альпи́йский, ‘Alpine’
-ль^{0}-ч-еск- [20+]		владе́лец, ‘an owner’; частновладе́льческий, ‘relating to private ownership’
-иан^{0}-ск- [15+]		Христо́с, ‘Christ’; христиа́нский, ‘Christian’
-ен^{0}-ск- [10+]		учрежде́ние, ‘an institution’; учрежде́нский, ‘relating to an institution’
-из-ат-ор-ск- [10+]		организова́ть, ‘to organize’; организа́торский, ‘organizer’s’
-ион-ер-ск- [10+]		мили́ция, ‘the police’; милицион́ерский, ‘policeman’s’
-ар-ск- [5+]		ле́карь (*m.*), ‘a physician’; ле́карский, ‘physician’s’
-ин^{1}-ск- [5+]		сатана́, ‘Satan’; satани́нский, ‘satanic’
-ит-ор-ск- [5+]		инквизи́ция, ‘an inquisition’; инквизи́торский, ‘inquisitor’s’
-ен^{0}-ск- [?]		бе́женец, ‘a refugee’; бе́женский, ‘refugee’s’ Пе́нза (the town of Penza); пе́нзенский, ‘Penza’
-СК [?] (WP)	I	брат, ‘a brother’; Братск (a new town in East Siberia)
СО- [50+] (NP)	I	преде́л, ‘a boundary’; сопреде́льный, ‘contiguous’
	I	оседа́ть, ‘to settle’; сосе́д, ‘a neighbour’
	II	звезда́, ‘a star’; созве́здие, ‘a constellation’
		See also С-

-СТВ-О (-*ЕСТВ-) [550+/360+] (P)	I	муж, ‘a husband, a man’ (*Poet.*); му́жество, ‘courage’
	I	лука́вый, ‘cunning’; лука́вство, ‘cunning’ (NP)
	II	крестья́нин, ‘a peasant’; крестья́нство, ‘the peasantry’
	III	производи́ть (*Ipf.*), ‘to produce’; произво́дство, ‘production’ (NP)
-тель^{0}-ств-о [120+]		вмеша́ть, ‘to interfere’; вмеша́тельство, ‘interference’
-нич-еств-о [100+]		сотру́дник, ‘a collaborator’; сотру́дничество, ‘collaboration’
-ов^{0}-ств-о [20+]		хва́статься, ‘to boast’; хвастовство́, ‘boastfulness’
-ат-ор-ств-о [15+]		дикта́т, ‘a dictate’; дикта́торство, ‘a dictatorship’
-ач-еств-о [15+]		чуда́к, ‘an eccentric’; чуда́чество, ‘eccentricity, oddness’
-ен^{0}-ств-о [15+]		пе́рвый, ‘first’; пе́рвенство, ‘a championship’
-иан-ств-о (-ьян-) [15+]		Ка́утский (the ideologist Kautsky); каутскиа́нство, ‘the ideas of Kautsky, Kautskyism’
-ч-еств-о [15+]		творе́ц, ‘a creator’; тво́рчество, ‘a creation, work; the act of creation’
-ёр-ств-о [10+]		доктри́на, ‘a doctrine’; доктринёрство, ‘doctrinaire views’
-ан-ств-о [5+]		Лю́тер (the theologian Luther); лютера́нство, ‘Lutheranism’
-ант-ств-о [5+]		протеста́нт, ‘a protestant’; протеста́нтство, ‘protestantism’
-ен^{0}-ч-еств-о [5+]		приспосо́бле́нец, ‘an opportunist’; приспосо́бле́нчество, ‘opportunism, time-serving’
-еч-еств-о [5+]		купе́ц, ‘a merchant’; купе́чество, ‘the merchant class’
-ин^{0}-ств-о [5+]		большо́й, ‘large’; большинство́, ‘a majority’
-ич-еств-о [5+]		като́лик, ‘a catholic’; католи́чество, ‘catholicism’
-ш^{0}-еств-о [5+]		но́вый, ‘new’; но́вшество, ‘a novelty’
СУ- [10+] (WP)	I	песо́к, ‘sand’; су́песок, ‘soil containing sand’; супесча́ный, ‘sandy, containing sand’
СУБ- [60+] (WP)	I	стратосфе́ра, ‘the stratosphere’; субстратосфе́ра, ‘the substratosphere’

	I подря́дчик, 'a contractor'; субподря́дчик, 'a sub-contractor'
СУПЕР- [10+] (WP)	I фосфа́т, 'phosphate'; суперфосфа́т, 'superphosphate' I обло́жка, 'an envelope, cover'; суперобло́жка, 'a jacket, dustcover, on a book'
-Т- [80+] (NP)	I смять (*Pf.*), 'to crumple'; смя́тый, 'crumpled'
-ТЕЛЬ [450+] (VP)	I гра́бить, 'to rob, despoil'; граби́тель, 'a thief, despoiler' I вая́ть, 'to model, sculpt'; вая́тель, 'a sculptor' II дви́гать, 'to move, propel'; дви́гатель, 'a motor' (P) II выключа́ть (*Ipf.*), 'to switch off'; выключа́тель, 'a switch' (P)
ТРАНС- (ТРАНСЪ-) [?] (WP)	I Сиби́рь, 'Siberia'; транссиби́рская ж. д., 'Trans-Siberian railway'
У- (*verbal*) [500+/5+]	ско́рый, 'quick'; уско́рить (*Pf.*), 'to accelerate'; ускоре́ние, 'acceleration' класть, 'to put, lay'; укла́дывать (*Ipf.*), 'to pack, stow away'; укла́дка, 'packing, stowing' ходи́ть, 'to go, walk'; уходи́ть (*Ipf.*), 'to go away'; ухо́д, 'departure' ходи́ть, 'to go, walk'; уха́живать (*Ipf.*), 'to care for; to court'; ухо́д, 'care, nursing'; уха́живание, 'courting'; ухажёр, 'a boy friend'
-у-по⁰- [5+]	ряд, 'a row'; поря́док, 'order'; упоря́доченный, 'put in order'
-УГ-А (-ЮГ-) [15+] (NP)	I бе́лый, 'white'; белу́га (a kind of sturgeon) I вить, 'to whirl, twist'; вьюга, 'a snowstorm' II по́длый, 'mean, despicable'; подлюга (*Pop.*), 'a despised person'
УЛЬТРА- [20+] (WP)	I ле́вый, 'left'; ультрале́вый, 'politically far to the left'
-УН [90+] (WP)	I лгать, 'to tell lies'; лгун, 'an habitual liar' I бе́гать, 'to run'; бегу́н, 'a runner, man who runs' II коло́ть, 'to split'; колу́н, 'an axe, chopper' (NP) III грызть, 'to gnaw'; грызу́н, 'a rodent' (NP)

-УР[1]-А [80+] (WP)	I литера́тор, 'a writer, man of letters'; литерату́ра, 'literature' I аге́нт, 'an agent'; агенту́ра, 'the activities of an agent' II аге́нт, 'an agent'; агенту́ра, 'a group of agents' II аспира́нт, 'a post-graduate student'; аспиранту́ра, 'a body of post-graduates'
-УР[2]-А [5+] (NP)	I ко́жа, 'skin'; кожура́, 'rind, peel'
-УХ (-ЮХ) [5+] (NP)	I ко́жа, 'skin'; кожу́х, 'a casing, housing' II петь, 'to sing'; пету́х, 'a cock'
-УХ-А (-ЮХ-) [50+] (WP)	I ста́рый, 'old'; стару́ха, 'an old woman' I горева́ть, 'to mourn, be sad'; горю́ха, 'a tearful person' II золото́й, 'golden'; золоту́ха, 'scrofula' (NP) II жёлтый, 'yellow'; желту́ха, 'jaundice' (NP)
-УЧ-	See -Ч-
-УШ-А (-КА) [15+] (WP)	I хло́пать, 'to flap, bang'; хлопу́шка, 'a fly swatter; a Christmas cracker; a pop-gun'
-УЩ- [5+] (NP)	I то́лстый, 'fat'; толсту́щий (*Pop.*), 'very fat' But see also -Щ-
-Ц-О [10+] (NP)	I крыло́, 'a wing'; крыльцо́, 'a porch'
-Ч- (-АЧ-, -УЧ-, -ЮЧ-, -ЯЧ-) [20+] (NP)	I коло́ть, 'to split, pierce'; колю́чая боль, 'a stabbing pain' I висе́ть, 'to be hanging'; вися́чий мост, 'a suspension bridge'
-Ч (-АЧ) [40+] (NP)	I ткать, 'to weave'; ткач, 'a weaver'
-ЧАК (-ч^{0}-ак?) [10+] (NP)	I весёлый, 'jolly'; весельча́к, 'a good-humoured, very jolly man' II зелёный, 'green'; зеленча́к, 'a green mushroom, a young plant'

-Ч-ЕЙ	See -АЙ
ЧЕРЕЗ- (ЧЕРЕС-) [5+] (NP)	I полоса́, 'a strip, stripe'; чересполо́сица, 'strip-farming' (cf. че́рез полосу́, 'every alternate strip') See also ЧРЕЗ-
-ЧИВ- [70+] (VP)	I заду́мываться (*Ipf.*), 'to be lost in thought'; заду́мчивый, 'pensive' I разобра́ть (*Pf.*), 'to distinguish, make out'; разбо́рчивый, 'clear, legible'
-ЧИК	See -ЩИК
-ЧИН-А	See -ЩИН-А
-ЧИЦ-А	See -ЩИЦ-А
ЧРЕЗ- [5+] (NP)	I обы́чай, 'a custom'; чрезвыча́йный, 'extraordinary' I ме́ра, 'a measure'; чрезме́рность, 'excessiveness' See also ЧЕРЕЗ-
-Ш- [20+] (NP)	I пасть (*Pf.*), 'to fall'; (падёт) па́дший, 'fallen'; па́дшие геро́и, 'fallen heroes'
-Ш-А [60+/30+] (P)	I дире́ктор, 'a director, a headmaster'; дире́кторша, 'a (specifically) woman director, a headmistress' II генера́л, 'a general'; генера́льша, 'a general's wife' (NP)
-ат-ор-ш-а [10+]	организова́ть, 'to organize'; организа́торша, 'an organizer' (*f.*)
-ёр-ш-а [10+]	контроли́ровать, 'to control'; контролёрша, 'an inspector' (*f.*)
-ор-ш-а [10+]	конду́ктор, 'a conductor, ticket-collector' (*m.*); конду́кторша, 'a conductor, ticket-collector' (*f.*)
-тель-ш-а [5+]	надзира́ть, 'to supervise'; надзира́тельша, 'a supervisor' (*f.*)
-Щ- (-АЩ-, -УЩ-, -ЮЩ-, -ЯЩ-) [180+] (P)	I подходи́ть (*Ipf.*), 'to be suitable'; подходя́щий, 'suitable, appropriate' I све́дать (*Pf. Arch.*), 'to find out, learn'; све́дущий, 'knowledgeable' (cf. ведь, 'surely; as you know')
-ЩИК (-ЧИК) [670+/280+] (P)	I ка́мень (*m.*), 'stone, a stone'; ка́менщик, 'a mason, a bricklayer' I газе́та, 'a newspaper'; газе́тчик, 'a newspaper seller; a journalist'

	I покупа́ть (*Ipf.*), 'to buy'; покупщи́к, 'a commercial buyer'
	I растра́тить (*Pf.*), 'to squander, embezzle'; растра́тчик, 'an embezzler'
	I жестяно́й, 'tin'; жестя́нщик (= жестя́ник), 'a maker of tin articles' (NP)
	I кладова́я, 'a pantry, a storeroom'; кладовщи́к, 'a storekeeper' (WP)
	II переда́ть, 'to transmit'; переда́тчик, 'a transmitting set' (WP)
	II счёт, 'a sum, an account'; счётчик, 'a meter, a counter'
-ль⁰-щик [200+]	носи́ть, 'to carry'; носи́льщик, 'a porter'
-ов²-щик (-ев-, -ёв-) [80+]	сверли́ть, 'to bore holes'; сверло́вщик, 'a drill operator'
-ЩИН-А (-ЧИН-) [100+/15+] (P)	I инозе́мный, 'foreign'; инозе́мщина (*Pop.*), 'foreign ways'
	I Обло́мов (Oblomov, a character in a novel by Goncharov); обло́мовщина, 'Oblomovism, passivity' (WP)
	II Волы́нь (the oblast of Volhynia); Волы́нщина (the area around this oblast, the Volhynia region) (WP)
-ль-щин-а [10+]	вида́ть, 'to see'; невида́льщина, 'something unheard of'
-аль-щин-а [5+]	теа́тр, 'a theatre'; театра́льщина, 'theatrical behaviour, theatrical nonsense'
-ЩИЦ-А (-ЧИЦ-) [170+/80+] (P)	I гардеро́бщик, 'a cloakroom attendant' (*m.*); гардеро́бщица, 'a cloakroom attendant' (*f.*)
	I буфе́тчик, 'a barman'; буфе́тчица, 'a barmaid'
-ль-щиц-а [80+]	ре́зать, 'to cut'; ре́зальщица, 'a cutter, cutting machine operator' (*f.*)
-ЫГ-А [5+] (NP)	I торопи́ться, 'to be in a hurry'; торопы́га (*Pop.*), 'a person who is always in a hurry'
-ЫНЬ [5+] (NP)	I све́тлый, 'light'; светлы́нь (*f.*) (*Pop.*), 'bright sunlight or moonlight' See also -ЫН-Я
-ЫН-Я (-ИН-) [30+] (NP)	I ба́рин, 'a gentleman, a landowner'; ба́рыня, 'a lady, the wife of a baron'

	I князь (*m.*), 'a prince'; княги́ня, 'a princess, the wife of a prince'
	II гусь (*m.*), 'a gander, a goose' (in general); гусы́ня, 'a goose' (*f.*)
	III пусто́й, 'empty'; пусты́ня, 'a desert'
	IV го́рдый, 'proud'; горды́ня, 'pride' (= го́рдость)
-ЫХ (-ИХ) [?] (NP)	I чёрный, 'black, dark'; Черны́х (the surname Chernykh)
-ЫШ (-ИШ) [40+/10+] (WP)	I го́лый, 'bare, naked'; голы́ш, 'a naked child; a pebble'
	II подки́нуть (*Pf.*), 'to abandon a child'; подки́дыш, 'an abandoned child'
	II вкладно́й, 'inserted, supplementary'; вкла́дыш, 'a supplement, something inserted'
	II вы́играть, 'to win'; вы́игрыш, 'winnings, an amount won'
-ён-ыш [10+]	гусь (*m.*), 'a goose, gander'; гусёныш (= гусёнок), 'a gosling'
*-Ь[1]- (= -ИЙ, -ЬЯ, -ЬЕ; -ЬИ) [30+/20+] (P)	I медве́дь (*m.*), 'a bear'; медве́жья берло́га, 'a bear's den'
	I деви́ца, 'a girl, a virgin'; деви́чья фами́лия, 'a maiden name'
	I стару́шка, 'an old woman'; стару́шечий го́лос, 'the voice of an old woman'
	I вдова́, 'a widow'; вдо́вий, 'belonging to a widow, proper to a widow' (NP)
	I поросёнок, 'a piglet'; порося́та, 'piglets'; порося́чий визг, 'the squealing of piglets' (NP)
	I ребёнок, 'a child'; ребя́чьи игру́шки, 'children's toys' (NP)
	II медве́дь (*m.*), 'a bear'; медве́жий, 'made of bearskin'
-нич-ь- [20+]	полко́вник, 'a colonel'; полко́вничий, 'colonel's'
-Ь[2], -Я, -Е [?] (NP)	I Яросла́в (the Christian name Yaroslav); Яросла́вль (an ancient town on the Volga)
*-ЬЕ (-ИЕ) [200+/2920+] (P)	I бе́рег, 'a bank, a coast'; побере́жье, 'the area along a river or coast, a littoral'
	I Кавка́з, 'the Caucasus'; Закавка́зье, 'Trans-Caucasus'
	I поля́рный, 'polar'; заполя́рье, 'the area beyond the Arctic circle.' (NP)
	II вели́кий, 'great'; вели́чие, 'grandeur'

	II	во́льный, 'free'; ду́мать, 'to think'; вольноду́мие, 'freethinking'
	II	плод, 'fruit'; беспло́дие, 'infertility'
-ен-ье (-ие) [1440+]		дели́ть, 'to divide'; деле́ние, 'division'
		сцепи́ть, 'to connect'; сцепле́ние, 'a connection'
-н-ье (-ие) [1320+]		поте́ть, 'to sweat'; поте́ние, 'sweating'
		восклица́ть, 'to cry out'; восклица́ние, 'an exclamation'
-т-ье (-ие) [100+]		закры́ть, 'to close'; закры́тие, 'closing'
		быть, 'to exist, be'; собы́тие, 'an event'
-ств-ие [40+]		беда́, 'ill-luck'; бе́дствие, 'a calamity'
-ов-ье [20+]		верх, 'a top'; верхо́вье, 'the upper reaches of a river'
*-ЬЁ [25+/20+] (WP)	I	сыро́й, 'raw'; сырьё, 'raw materials'
	I	зверь (*m.*), 'an animal'; зверьё (*Pop.*), 'a number of animals, animals in general'
	II	чу́ткий, 'sensitive'; чутьё, 'a flair'; языково́е чутьё, 'a feeling for language' (NP)
-т-ьё [15+]		бить, 'to beat'; битьё, 'beating, a beating'
-н-ьё [10+]		врать, 'to exaggerate, lie'; враньё, 'exaggeration, fibs'
-Ь-Я (-УН-Ь-Я) [60+] (NP)	I	говору́н, 'a talkative man'; говору́нья, talkative woman'
ЭКС- [5+] (P)	I	председа́тель, 'a chairman'; экс-председа́тель, 'an ex-chairman'
-ЮГ-А		See -УГ-А
-ЮХ		See -УХ
-ЮХ-А		See -УХ-А
-ЮЧ-		See -Ч-
-ЮЩ-		See -Щ-
-ЯВ- (-АВ-) [20+/10+] (NP)	I	ку́дри, 'curls'; кудря́вый, 'curly-headed'
	*I	мо́лод, 'young'; моложа́вый, 'of youthful appearance'
$-л^0$-яв- [10+]		верте́ть, 'to turn'; вертля́вый, 'fidgety, unable to keep still'
		мозги́, 'brains, intelligence'; мозгля́вый, 'overpensive, timid'

-ЯГ-А [30+] (WP)	I рабо́тать, 'to work'; работя́га, 'a really hard worker' I до́брый, 'good, kind'; добря́га (*Pop.*), 'a very kind-hearted person' II двор, 'a yard'; дво́рный, 'domestic, belonging to the yard' (*Arch.* = дворо́вый); дворня́га, 'a dog kept out of doors' (NP)
-ЯЙ	See -АЙ
-ЯК(-А)	See -АК(-А)
-ЯН- (-АН-) [20+] (WP)	I жесть (*f.*), 'tinplate'; жестяно́й, 'tin' I ко́жа, 'leather'; ко́жаный, 'leather' II дрова́, 'logs'; дровяно́й склад, 'a stock of wood; a woodshed' (NP)
-ЯН	See -АН
-ЯНН-	See -ЕНН-
-ЯР	See -АР
-ЯСТ-	See -АСТ-
-ЯЧ-	See -Ч-
-ЯШ (-АШ) [5+] (NP)	I до́брый, 'good, kind'; добря́ш (*Pop.*), 'a benefactor'
ЯЩ-	See -Щ-

e (Diminutive/Augmentative) Affixes

In addition to affixes expressing as objective meanings either diminution (-ЁН-ОК, МИКРО-, and to a lesser degree ПОД-, СУБ-) or augmentation (-ЕНН- (II), МАКРО-, НАИ-, ПРЕ-, -УЩ-, -ЧАК, and to a lesser degree ДО-), there exist in Russian a number of suffixes used to express not only variety in size but also the attitude of the speaker or writer to the object in question. The emotive content may be dominant (as in звёздочка, 'a dear little star') or the idea of large or small size may be equally prominent (as in ту́мбочка, 'a small stool'). In a minority of cases the emotive content is weakened through polysemanticization (as in ка́рточка, 'a postcard / visiting-card / filing card / snapshot') and, rarely, the implication of affection or dislike is altogether lost (as in була́вка, 'a pin'; cf. булава́, 'a mace').

A list of suffixes expressing emotive meaning, in addition to variety in size, is given below. Those forms which may also express non-emotive (objective) lexical meanings and which are included in the main list above are marked with a double asterisk.

-АН-ЁК
-АШ-К-А
-ЕВ-АТ-ЕНЬ-К-
-ЕН-ЁК
**-ЕНН-
-ЕНЬ-К-
-ЕНЬ-К-А
**-ЕЦ
-ЕЦ-О
-ЕЧ-К-О
-ЁК
**-ЁН-К-А
-ЁН-К-И
-ЁХ-ОНЬ-К-
-ЁШ-ЕНЬ-К-
-ЁШ-К-А
**-ИК
-ИК-О
**-ИН-А
**-ИН-К-А
**-ИЦ-А
-ИЦ-Е
-ИШ-ЕЧ-К-
-ИШ-К-
-ИЩ-А
**-ИЩ-Е
**-К-А
**-К-О
-ОВ-АТ-ЕНЬ-К-
**-ОК
-ОН-К-А
-ОН-ОЧ-К-
-ОНЬ-К-
-ОНЬ-К-А
-ОХ-ОНЬ-К-
-ОЧ-ЕК
-ОЧ-К-А
-ОШ-ЕНЬ-К-
-УШ-ЕК
-УШ-ЕЧ-К-
-УШ-ЕЧ-К-А
-УШ-К-
**-УШ-К-А
**-УЩ-
-Ц-А
-Ц-Е
**-Ц-О
**-ЧИК
-ЫШ-ЕК
-ЫШ-К-О
-ЮШ-К-
**-ЮЩ-
-ЯТ-К-О

BIBLIOGRAPHY

A. *Books referred to in this work*

Academy Grammar = *Грамматика русского языка.* 3 vols., АН СССР, Moscow, 1952–4. (Revised reprint, 1960.) (A collective work.)

Bielfeldt, H. H. (ed.). *Rückläufiges Wörterbuch der Russischen Sprache der Gegenwart.* Akademie-Verlag, Berlin, 1958. (2nd ed. 1965.)

Entwistle, W. J. and Morison, W. A. *Russian and the Slavonic Languages.* Faber, London, 1949.

Jespersen, O. *A Modern English Grammar* (vol. 6). Carl Winter, Heidelberg, 1922, and George Allen and Unwin, London, 1949 (and later editions).

Koritsky, B. F. (ed.). *Словарь сокращений русского языка.* ГИИНС, Moscow, 1963.

Maruzo (Marouzeau), Zh. *Словарь лингвистических терминов.* Издательство иностранной литературы, Moscow, 1960.

Ozhegov, S. I. and Shapiro, A. B. (eds.). *Орфографический словарь русского языка.* ГИИНС, Moscow, 1957 (and later editions).

Scheitz, E. *Russische Abkürzungen und Kurzwörter.* VEB Verlag, Berlin, 1961.

Shteinfeldt, E. A. *Частотный словарь русского языка.* Tallinn, 1963.

Ushakov, D. N. (ed.) *Толковый словарь русского языка.* 4 vols., Объединение государственных издательств, Moscow, 1935–40.

B. *For further reading*

Muchnik, I. P. and Panov, M. V. (eds.). *Развитие грамматики и лексики современного русского языка.* Наука, Moscow, 1964. [Contains six articles on word formation which describe some of the most recent developments.]

Vinogradov, V. V. (ed.). *Изменения в словообразовании и формах существительного и прилагательного в русском литературном языке.* In *Очерки по исторической грамматике русского литературного языка XIX в.* Наука, Moscow, 1964. [A very detailed description of changes in the use of the more common affixes in the period 1700–1900.]

Zemskaya, E. A. *Как делаются слова.* АН СССР, Moscow, 1963. [A short and clearly written introduction to the subject.]